Q 87 S13 15

Getting Reading Started

Getting Reading Started

Dolores Durkin
University of Illinois

Allyn and Bacon, Inc.
Boston London Sydney Toronto

Portions of this book first appeared in *Teaching Young Children To Read,* Third Edition, by Dolores Durkin, copyright © 1980, 1976, 1972 by Allyn and Bacon, Inc.

Library of Congress Cataloging in Publication Data

Durkin, Dolores.
   Getting reading started.

   Includes bibliographical references and index.
   1. Reading readiness. 2. Reading (Preschool)
I. Title
LB1140.5.R4D87   372.4   81–8012
ISBN 0–205–07559–2   AACR2

Printed in the United States of America

10 9 8 7 6 5   87 86 85

Contents

Part II
Early Instructional Programs   79

Part III
Early Instructional Materials   187

Preface

When reading instruction began to make its way into kindergartens in the 1960s, too much of it seemed inappropriate for five-year-olds. Visits to classrooms, for instance, pointed up programs marked by such questionable features as whole-class instruction, a dependence on commercial materials, and the use of drill and numerous ditto sheets. At times, concern about the children's readiness for the instruction being offered appeared to be nonexistent.

To help counteract that development, I wrote *Teaching Young Children to Read,* which was published in 1972. Essentially, it represented an attempt to show with many illustrations how kindergartners (and nursery school children) who are ready can be eased—not pushed—into reading in ways that make the experience personal, interesting, successful, and nonthreatening. How to help unready children to get ready also was dealt with.

Although the response to *Teaching Young Children to Read* was positive, some educators said that its content was too circumscribed to be suitable for reading methodology courses that cover kindergarten through grade three. For this reason, the second edition, which became available in 1976, had a broader focus.

The response to the second edition continued to be positive; but now, early childhood educators said that the new version told their students more than they needed to know for their work with four-, five-, and six-year-old children. What to do?

To accommodate as many educators as possible, decisions were made, first, to prepare a third edition of *Teaching Young Children to Read* that would retain the kindergarten–grade three focus, and, second, to make available a shorter book composed of those chapters in the third edition that are directed specifically to early childhood educators. *Getting Reading Started* is the product of the second decision. Except for the Introduction and final chapter, all the material appears in *Teaching Young Children to Read.*

Getting Reading Started is meant to help teachers and aides in nursery schools, day-care centers, Head Start programs, kindergartens, and first grades. It is especially aimed at those educators who believe that *some* pre-first-grade children are ready to read and that teaching them is not just a matter of imitating first-grade programs. It is also for those people who recognize that other pre-first graders are not ready for reading and that one professional responsibility is to help them become ready. Most of all, *Getting Reading Started* should show that readiness and reading instruction can be enjoyable activities for teachers and children alike.

Since about 98 percent of teachers of young children are women, feminine pronouns are used in the text to refer to teachers. (This practice also avoids awkward expressions such as "she or he".) In contrast, reference to a child will use "he" unless a specific girl is the referent. This is done to avoid ambiguity when a pronoun for a teacher and another for a child are used in the same sentence.

D. D.

Introduction

In decades gone by, the professional preparation of teachers of young children routinely omitted attention to reading instruction except perhaps to advise, "Don't do anything with it!" At least two reasons account for the omission. One was the prevailing views about what affects a child's growth and development. (These views will be discussed in Chapter 3.) The other reason stemmed from the belief that reading instruction is inevitably bound up with an amount of structure and formalization that early childhood educators did not think was desirable for young children. Omitting reading, therefore, was seen as a way to ensure that the value of things like play and creativity would continue to be appreciated as teachers planned how their time and the children's would be spent.

Then came new and even radically different theories about the potential of young children and, further, about the unique importance of the first five years of life for their eventual intellectual growth. (These theories, too, are referred to in Chapter 3.) One consequence was widespread interest in doing everything earlier, including teaching reading. Whether they wanted to or not, therefore, many kindergarten teachers found themselves in a position where they were expected to do something with reading. In certain communities, nursery school teachers experienced similar expectations.

Unfortunately, the demands came into existence at a time when, for reasons mentioned earlier, the majority of early childhood teachers were unprepared to teach reading. Since neither the schools themselves nor colleges and universities provided the kind of help that was needed, whatever was available landed in kindergartens: workbooks and ditto sheets. Because most of the workbooks dealt with phonics, so, too, did most of the reading instruction. It was thus natural that all the old worries about the effect of reading instruction on early childhood programs were resurrected. In some cases, in fact, opposition to earlier reading was as vocal as it had been in prior decades. In too few cases, on the other hand, was any effort made to show how reading ability can be initiated in ways that will not have a negative effect either on programs or on children.

While all these developments were occurring, I was conducting long-term research that has greatly influenced my own thinking about young children and reading. In fact, findings from these studies account in part for *Getting Reading Started.*

RESEARCH WITH PRESCHOOL READERS

The initial research was composed of two studies of children who learned to read at home prior to entering school (1). Begun in 1958, the research was carried out at a time when early home help with reading was frowned on as much as, or more than, kindergarten help. Although the two studies took place in locations that were separated by almost 3,000 miles, findings were strikingly similar.

To begin, age four was the most common time for an interest in written language to become apparent. Children often displayed it with questions like, "What does that sign say?" or "Where does it say that?" Sometimes, too, interest became visible through an expressed desire to learn to print. Requests and questions like "Make me my name" and "How do you make a *b*?" were often referred to by parents during home interviews.

What also became clear as parents responded to interview questions is that the early readers came from homes in which people read. All the children had been read to regularly, for instance, sometimes from a very early age. In addition, at least one parent was described, if not as an avid reader, at least as a frequent reader.

Parents of the early readers also turned out to be individuals who seemed to have enjoyed their young children; who frequently took them places; and who spent time discussing and naming what had been seen, answering questions, and stimulating still more. Much oral and written language, therefore, was an integral part of the early readers' lives and environment.

Deliberate attempts by parents to teach their preschoolers to read were rare. Instead, their help tended to be responses to the children's own questions and requests. If any "instructional materials" did exist in homes, they were pencils and paper and small chalkboards. Also influential was whatever had been read to the children—trade books, encyclopedia articles, comics, and so on. Other materials that aroused curiosity about print included calendars; newspaper headlines; menus; directions for playing games or for making something; labels on canned goods, packages, and boxes; and television commercials and weather reports. ("Sesame Street" had not yet come into existence.)

As is indicated by these and other of the findings, the two studies of early readers showed that a "language arts approach" is an apt description of the "instructional programs" that went on at home.* Stimulating growth in both oral and written language abilities were various combinations of (a) a literate environment; (b) adult models who read; (c) interesting experiences that were discussed; (d) availability of someone who answered questions and responded to requests related to reading, writing, and spelling; (e) availability of materials for writing; and (f) positive contacts with books and reading.

---

* *Language Arts* is an educational term that refers to listening, speaking, reading, and writing.

RESEARCH WITH SCHOOL PROGRAM

Since it appeared that the children had *enjoyed* becoming readers and writers and since the data that were collected over a six-year period showed anything but negative effects on achievement in reading, subsequent plans were made for a third study: the development of a two-year language arts program that would start with four-year-old children (2, 3). The objective of the experiment was to assemble a curriculum that would resemble the language arts "program" in the homes of the early readers. The hope was for new insights about appropriate ways to teach beginning reading in school. Because a second objective was to compare over time the reading ability of the children in the program with that of other children who did not receive initial instruction in reading until first grade, the research continued (with regularly scheduled classroom observations and periodic testing) until the end of fourth grade. Starting with first grade, what was done with reading was determined by the public school that both groups of children attended.

FINDINGS

Since what occurred during the two-year experimental program enters into all the chapters in *Getting Reading Started,* only some of what resulted will be mentioned here.

One clear result for the researcher was a new appreciation for the learning potential of four- and five-year-old children. Admittedly, their "littleness" was somewhat intimidating at first. The group of thirty-nine—some of whom had not yet had a fourth birthday when the program began—did prompt reflections like, "Why in the world am I thinking about reading for these very young children?" Soon, though, the most prominent characteristic was not their "littleness" but rather their zest, curiosity, and success in learning. Equally apparent during all of the two years of the experimental program was the attractiveness of anything that related to the children themselves. That teachers of young children should make maximum use of their experiences and interests now seems unquestionable.

While none of the children were experts in reading at the end of the two-year program, all had acquired some ability. What stood out after the final testing was the wide range in what had been learned (3). But this outcome should have been expected since every effort had been made to avoid boredom for the fast learners and frustration for the slower ones.

Because all of the children in the program *could* do some reading, it was surprising that they still had to take a reading readiness test when they entered first grade. After all, is there any better evidence of readiness for reading than the ability to do some? Especially interesting about the results of the testing is that certain children who could read did less well on the test than others who had not participated in the program and could not read. Why this was so is probably rooted in the fact that children not in the program had attended a kindergarten in which readiness instruction centered on readiness workbooks. Since both the format and content of the workbooks closely resembled the format and content of the test, it is highly likely that use of the former prepared for the latter. Whatever the explanation, test results certainly raised questions about readiness tests. So, too, did the progress of the two groups in reading during the next four years.

For each of the four years that reading achievement was compared, the children who had participated in the experimental program were more advanced than the group who had not. (The two groups were statistically matched on intelligence for each comparison.) To be noted, however, is that the difference in achievement was smaller at the end of fourth grade than it had been at the conclusion of first grade (3). But that was predictable for the following reason.

Starting in first grade and continuing until fourth grade, instructional materials in the public school were assigned not in relation to reading ability but on the basis of grade-level placement. This meant that when children from the experimental program started first grade, all—even the most advanced in reading—were given beginning materials. At the start of second grade, the same procedure was followed: nobody received anything more difficult than a second-grade reader. And the same pattern continued for the next two grades. While it would be less than accurate to say that *no* effort was made to provide individualized instruction,* it is very accurate to state that what was taught was affected much more by commercial materials than by what the children

---

* As used in this book, *individualized instruction* refers to any instruction that deals with what a child or a group needs and is ready to learn, proceeding in a way and at a pace that is suitable for the individual or group being instructed.

could and could not do. One consequence is that the research was unable to reach valid conclusions about the later consequences of earlier starts in reading *when* the earlier starts are taken advantage of in subsequent years.

What the research *is* able to point to are some thoughts for any educator responsible for making a decision about when to initiate reading instruction:

● No school should introduce reading instruction into the kindergarten unless it is able and willing to alter its first-grade program in ways that will use and extend what is learned in kindergarten.

● No school should have reading in the kindergarten unless and until the kindergarten teacher is fully prepared to teach it in ways that are appropriate for five-year-olds.

● To facilitate individualized instruction, what children learn in kindergarten should be communicated to the first-grade teacher in some highly specific form. This will allow her to know where to begin.

Two other points do not derive from the research but, nonetheless, are important to keep in mind when decisions about the timing of reading instruction are being made:

● The only defensible reason for initiating reading instruction in kindergarten is the conviction that some or all of the children are ready for it.

Children who turn out to be unready should receive readiness instruction, since individualized instruction is just as necessary at the kindergarten level as it is at any other.

● Only kindergarten teachers who are fully prepared to teach reading in ways that are suitable for young children are in a position to make valid judgments about readiness. This is so because when unprepared teachers decide that children are not ready, their judgment may reflect their own insecurity as much as it does the children's lack of readiness. Teachers who equate teaching reading with drill and workbooks are not in a good position to make judgments, either, because their conclusions might reflect negative feelings about an undesirable methodology as much as they do an objective assessment of abilities.

With these various reminders in the background, let's now begin to consider how young children can be eased into reading in ways that add to both their enjoyment and their self-esteem.

REFERENCES

1. Durkin, Dolores. *Children Who Read Early*. New York: Teachers College Press, 1966.
2. Durkin, Dolores. "A Language Arts Program for Pre-First Grade Children: Two Year Achievement Report." *Reading Research Quarterly* V (Summer, 1970), 534–565.
3. Durkin, Dolores. "A Six Year Study of Children Who Learned to Read in School at the Age of Four." *Reading Research Quarterly* X (1974–75, No. 1), 9–61.

I

At the Beginning

Not too many years ago, school instruction in reading for children younger than six was unheard of—or if such a possibility was mentioned, responses were anything but supportive. Then came the 1960s with its new theories and hypotheses about the special significance of a child's first five years of life for intellectual development. Even though documented facts were lacking, everyone was soon scurrying about looking for ways to provide children with earlier intellectual stimulation.

That such an interest fostered changed attitudes toward pre–first grade starts in reading was only natural. After all, an era that assigned critical importance to learning opportunities during the early years was not likely to be patient with school practices that postponed reading instruction beyond the start of first grade on the assumption that the passing of time automatically ensured a readiness for it. One result of all these shifts and changes is that kindergarten reading is now common. Even directors of nursery schools and day-care centers wonder whether their children might be ready to be readers.

Unquestionably, some of the actual reasons why particular schools are trying to teach reading before first grade are indefensible. I refer to reasons such as the desire to keep up with other schools, the desire to look up-to-date, and the willingness to succumb to parental pressure even when children would profit more from something other than reading instruction. Whether the reason is defensible or indefensible, the fact is that earlier reading programs are here. Therefore, professional educators must do whatever they can to ensure that what is done with reading is suitable for younger children.

The first step in carrying out such a responsibility is to learn what younger children are like. Descriptions of what they are like in classrooms provide the content for Chapter 1. What their teachers are like is described in Chapter 2.

A look at both children and teachers is necessary for a consideration of readiness for reading (the topic of Chapter 3) because whether any child succeeds with beginning reading depends as much on the kind and quality of instruction that is offered as it does on the child's abilities. By the time you finish Chapters 1–3, therefore, you should understand all that's involved in answering the question, *Is* this child ready to begin to read?

CHAPTER

1

Behavioral Characteristics of Young Children in Classrooms

PREVIEW

Ideally, the material for Chapter 1 would have come from many carefully executed studies of the behavior of young children in classrooms. The children would have varied in chronological age, intelligence, sex, race, and home background. They would have attended schools with varying philosophies regarding the education of young children and, therefore, with varying goals and curricula. And their teachers would have differed in such relevant factors as professional preparation, number of years of teaching, age, sex, personality, and expectations regarding behavior and learnings. Unfortunately, such research is still to be done. That is why this chapter is based on what I myself have learned while observing in countless numbers of nursery school, kindergarten, and first-grade classrooms.

When first observing, I had no idea that what I was seeing would become material for a teacher's textbook. However, the more I visited classrooms (and I have been in schools in a variety of geographical and socioeconomic areas) the more I began to realize that children of these age levels share certain characteristics that ought to be taken into account by anyone who works with them. Some of the characteristics make that work uniquely rewarding; others, uniquely difficult and challenging. In either case, teachers should know about the characteristics and keep them in mind as they plan schedules and instruction and make decisions about important matters like goals and materials.

As you read Chapter 1, bear in mind that it is based on the observations of one person—me. For that reason, be sure to compare what is said about young children with what *you* know about them. Such comparisons should add to your comprehension of the chapter as well as to your knowledge of young children.

To enhance comprehension, you might also want to take a look at the questions found at the end of the chapter before you begin to read it. They are found under the heading "Review."

As behavioral characteristics are discussed in this chapter, none are labeled as being especially pronounced at a specific age. That is the case because I have learned from classroom visits that the behavior of some fours is like that of some sixes, that the behavior of some sixes is not yet up to that of some fours, and so on. This is not to deny that a group of six-year-olds, as a whole, will be more mature and able than a group of fours. However, the job of a teacher is to deal with individuals. And individually, children of the same age differ greatly. For that reason, the characteristics discussed in this chapter are viewed as being common among young children; but there is no pretense about their adding up to a description of every young child.

Because my own research has given me the chance to learn about young children's behavior with parents as well as with teachers, there can also be no assumption that behavior is the same at home as it is in school. That parents and teachers treat the children differently is one reason for the variation. The extent of such differences was brought to my attention somewhat dramatically. I had been visiting in a nursery school and was especially impressed with one girl's mature behavior and advanced learnings. Physically, she was the smallest in the group, but she was certainly the "biggest" in the way she behaved and in how easily she learned everything. That was why I was surprised—even shocked—by what happened when her mother arrived at dismissal time. The mother met her at the door, picked her up as if she were about a year old, and carried her to a nearby car. My immediate thought: "I wonder how that child behaves at home."

In another case, I came to know a four-year-old boy quite well. At school, his behavior was so docile that I once commented to his teacher, "I think if you told that child to jump out the window, he would." According to his mother, however, he was willful at home, had frequent temper tantrums when he didn't get his own way, and spent most nights sleeping on the living room sofa because of his refusal to stop watching television.

The comment of still another mother is worth quoting. Speaking about her son, who was then in first grade, she noted, "Why, when his teacher talks about him, it's as if she's describing a child I don't even know!"

What follows are descriptions of young children as they behaved in classrooms only.

TRADITIONAL TEACHINGS VERSUS OBSERVED BEHAVIOR

That we often see what we expect to see cannot be forgotten in a chapter concerned with descriptions of behavior based on classroom observations. Although the earliest of the observations were not made in order to examine behavior, it is still likely that I had certain expectations based on what I had read or heard or what I had been taught in early childhood education courses.

What I had been taught about the characteristics of young children was cited by educators as being reasons for keeping reading out of the kindergarten. Therefore, these traditional teachings are highly relevant for a book called *Teaching Young Children to Read*. Some of the most influential of the earlier contentions are stated below:

1. Young children have difficulty relating to more than one adult.
2. Young children require a daily rest period.
3. Young children have short attention spans.
4. Young children have great need for help with social and emotional development; in fact, promotion of such development is the primary reason for having them go to school.

A discussion of each of these traditional teachings in relation to observed behavior follows.

Do Young Children Have Difficulty Relating to More Than One Adult?

In the majority of classes visited there was only one adult, the teacher. It might be relevant, therefore, to comment about the reactions of the children to me, an adult visitor who in most instances was a stranger.

How the children reacted probably was affected by the role I played—or tried to play. My intention was to be an unobtrusive visitor who did not get in the way of the teacher or the children. Thus, I made no effort to communicate with either or to become part of what they were doing. The children, nonetheless, went out of their way to include me.

Typically, when I first entered a room the children looked at me, but if any caught my eye, they quickly turned away as if shy and self-conscious. Within a short time, however, I became an object for study. Later, when the children were used to my being in the room, a child would come over to show me something: a toy or paper or, perhaps, new shoes. Even when I made only a minimal response, others soon came to me, too. If, as I tended to do when just a neophyte observer, I made a positive comment about what was shown, then many children inevitably brought me something. There were times, in fact, when I had to tell them I could not talk.

As the sequence of responses described above occurred over and over, forming a pattern, it became clear that for the children, the second adult was a potential source of extra attention and praise and, therefore, a welcome addition to the classroom. Whenever teaching assistants were available, they seemed to have the same value. Children were eager to be with them, to have their attention, and to win their approval.

To sum up: Based on my observations, it seems that the more adults there are, the better children like it. In fact, I saw *no* evidence of young children having difficulty relating to more than one. There were, to be sure, individual children who were extremely shy and found it hard to approach anyone. However, whenever I had the chance to visit frequently in classrooms that had these children, they too—but still shyly—eventually came to show or tell me something. Once the initial contact was made, future "visits" usually were common.

Do Young Children Require a Daily Rest Period?

One four-year-old that I am acquainted with attends a day-care center. A bus picks him up each morning shortly before seven o'clock and returns him in the evening just after six o'clock. I refer to this child immediately because his need for a rest period seems unquestionable. What he really should have, in fact, is a good long nap on a comfortable bed.

What about children who attend half-day programs? Do they also need to nap in school?

Daily rest periods were scheduled in the nursery schools and kindergartens that I visited, but not in the first grades. This traditional practice seemed to assume great differences between five- and six-year-olds, for the fives attended school for half a day and were given a rest period, whereas the sixes went to school for a full day and were not. Did my many observations lead to support for, or rejection of, such an assumption?

What the observations led to was an awareness that the so-called rest period was anything but restful. Usually, children were asked to lie on the floor on some type of mat or rug. Often, but not always, quiet music was played, and the window shades were drawn. Almost inevitably, though, the children wiggled or talked or bothered a neighbor. Frequently, a teacher had to discipline individuals. If, by chance, she named unacceptable behavior ("Kim, keep your hands to yourself"), it inevitably spread among the children, and further scoldings and admonitions followed. Conclusion? As typically carried out, rest periods provide little rest for the children and still less for their teachers.

Because of what had been observed in so many classrooms, certain teachers were urged to omit rest periods and, instead, to alter their schedules to provide relaxing changes of pace: quiet periods followed by more active ones, and concentrated activities followed by more relaxed types. Teachers were also reminded of the need to provide outlets for young children's tremendous—sometimes unbelievable—energy. Influenced by the current interest in physical fitness, one kindergarten teacher introduced a brief period of calisthenics each day. Only one child, a chubby girl, objected because, "These exercises bend me too much."

To deny the need for regularly scheduled rest periods is not also to say that children were never tired. Indeed they were. During one of my first visits to kindergarten classrooms, a boy fell asleep fairly early in the morning while the teacher was reading a story. She said later that he was always tired, but this was the first time he actually slept. Listening to a large number of comments in many rooms made it clear that far too many young children watch television late into the evening. This became evident when they referred to programs that ended at ten o'clock and even later.

Insufficient rest, then, is not rare and can be a problem; but the rest periods still scheduled in nursery schools and kindergartens probably are not helping. Certainly they are not helping in communities where it is common for large numbers of children to come to school not only tired but also hungry. What must be recognized in these areas is, first, that basic physical needs must be taken care of before other goals are considered; and, second, that the traditional rest period combined with the equally traditional juice and cracker are hardly sufficient to take care of basic needs.

Do Young Children Have Short Attention Spans?

One commonly held view of young children is that they have *very* short attention spans. In contrast to this, my observations revealed that the length of time they give to anything is affected by a great many variables. I would therefore like to suggest that general statements describing the attention span of a group or even of an individual do not reflect the realities of life in classrooms.

To be specific, when the attention spans of individuals of the same age and in the same class were compared, they always varied—sometimes considerably. Complicating the comparisons was the fact that for each child, a single description or judgment was often inaccurate. Here I cannot help but recall a boy in a kindergarten I visited regularly. In general, I had classified him as a hop-skip-and-jumper, for when allowed to do so, he flitted from one thing to another. Yet, put paper in front of him and crayons in his hands, and he was a different child—or so it seemed. Always the last to finish an art project, this boy produced meticulously executed pictures.

Curious about the ever-present details in his art work, I once talked with him about a picture he had drawn of his parents. From the conversation, I learned that he had taken the time to curl his mother's hair, to make her dress a floral print, and to put gloves on her hands and bows on her shoes. Naturally, she was carrying a nicely detailed purse. And with his father he had been just as careful: best hat with band and a tiny feather, handkerchief in suitcoat pocket, wide stripes in tie, and laces in shoes.

Had another visitor gone into the classroom at any time other than the art period, she or he would have assigned descriptions like "giddy" and "restless" to that child's behavior. If observing only during art, however, the same person would have been impressed by the steady, patient attention this boy gave to his work. While the work and play of other children in that classroom were not char-acterized by such extremes, it was still difficult—and also inaccurate—to label the attention span of each with a single description. More correct and realistic is the contention that each had a collection of attention spans.

Observations indicated that a child has a collection of attention spans for some of the same reasons that an adult has a collection. Factors such as fatigue, illness, and mood, for instance, play important roles. In fact, in classrooms that were visited regularly over a period of a year or more, the relevance of children's moods became especially pronounced. Some children, of course, were far less moody than others, but all had their good days and bad days. I often thought that wet weather brought out everyone's bad mood; whenever there was a series of rainy days, there usually was a great deal of restlessness, too.

Other factors had a positive effect on the amount of time children were will-ing to give to something. If an activity related to the children themselves or at least had a connection with what was familiar, it was likely to get and keep their attention. Too, if previous involvement with something had led to achievement or praise, that activity was likely to succeed in involving them again. Also suc-cessful in holding the children's attention was whatever they themselves selected. When teachers kept such factors as these in mind when they planned a day's activities, an observer could be nothing but impressed with the way children be-came involved and stayed involved. It was in these classrooms in particular that traditional teachings about the short attention span of a young child seemed highly questionable.

While there were innumerable times when I was pleasantly surprised at the sustained attention of four-, five-, and six-year-old children, there were other times when I was equally surprised at how easily they could be distracted—and this was true even of the older-acting ones.

The greatest distraction, I learned, is another child. If left alone, an individ-ual might stay with something for what seemed like an endless amount of time. But then along would come a friend, and the picture changed. The more I ob-served the more I also noticed that in just about every classroom, at least one boy or girl spent a considerable amount of time interrupting children who were busy and occupied.

Other common distractions are new acquisitions. Once I observed a boy with new cowboy boots and a girl with a new watch turn into intermittent sources of distraction for a whole day. At other times, in other classrooms, irresistible attractions were bracelets (especially those that dangle), bandages, combs, rings, and jewelry pins. On one occasion I learned that even a piece of string could get in the way of a peaceful morning in school.

To sum up, then, classroom observations uncovered variety rather than uni-formity in attention spans. Such variety was characteristic not only between chil-dren but also within a single child. What seems to be an accurate conclusion, therefore, is that children have a collection of attention spans, each determined by many factors that work together to affect its depth as well as its length.

Should Social and Emotional Development Be the Major Goal of School Programs for Young Children?

Traditionally, a child's social and emotional development has been of major concern to educators responsible for planning pre–first grade programs. Consequently, goals like emotional stability, self-acceptance, independence, and ability to get along with others have been emphasized for nursery schools and kindergartens. The question to consider now is, Did visits to pre–first grade classrooms verify the need for such emphases?

To be stressed immediately is that classroom observations are not a prerequisite for appreciating both the importance and the necessity of helping young children with various aspects of what might globally be called good mental health. One merely has to be alive to know there is always room for growth in this area whether a person is a child or an adult. Therefore, the need to justify concern about a young child's social and emotional development is nonexistent.

What still remains questionable is the traditionalist's tendency to artificially separate social and emotional goals from academic or intellectual ones. A question about this is raised because the unfortunate result of that tendency has been either-or thinking and, therefore, either-or decisions. Should we emphasize getting along with others, or should we be teaching readiness for reading? Should we help a child grow in independence, or should we introduce simple mathematical concepts? These were the kinds of either-or questions that were asked, and traditional answers moved in the direction of the social and emotional goals.

What classroom observations suggest is that goals like these should not be isolated, as has been traditionally done, because they are not achieved in isolation. That is, they are not attained in a vacuum but, rather, as children participate in activities connected with other goals.

Why traditionalists have given such special—though, unfortunately, isolated—attention to social and emotional goals is made clear during classroom visits, especially when they occur close to the start of the children's first year in school. It is then that matters like "learning to be a good group member" seem to be of crucial importance. But even (perhaps especially) at that time, it must be recognized that such learnings are never *achieved* if by that word one means *fully and permanently realized*. As adults we ought to be keenly aware that the many goals that have been named in the past by early childhood educators (e.g., emotional stability, social adjustment) are only rarely achieved to the fullest even in the most mature of adults. Consequently, to hold them up as goals for young children is not reasonable. The assumption of this book is that social and emotional goals are achieved gradually in conjunction with academic goals. For certain young children, the latter should include the ability to do some reading. It is further assumed that a lack of intellectual stimulation in school programs may create behavior problems, which, in turn, make children seem less mature and adjusted than they really are.

OTHER COMMONLY OBSERVED CHARACTERISTICS

Characteristics other than those mentioned were observed often enough to be named. Probably the most obvious were curiosity and self-interest, traits that have such potential and universality that they have prompted a great many of the recommendations in later chapters. Other noticeable characteristics were excitability, imagination, imitation, suggestibility, impatience, misuse of words, self-awareness, independence, enjoyment of challenges, and nonpredictability.

Excitability

The tendency of young children to get excited about anything and everything became very apparent as classrooms were visited. The source of excitement could be icy sidewalks, a child's loose tooth, or a birthday party scheduled for after school. It did not have to be of monumental importance; young children are interested in many things, and with their interest comes their excitement.

Teachers accustomed to working with the older and more blasé child would consider it a treat to get the response that is common for those who teach the young ones. What a joy, for instance, when children get excited because a teacher decides to use last names for attendance-taking rather than the customary first names. How rewarding, too, when children get excited because they suddenly see in books words they can read: *go, the, some.* Equally refreshing is the enjoyment they find in acting out the meanings of words—*jump* and *hop,* for instance.

While this easily aroused excitement has obvious rewards for teachers, it has its problems, too. A teacher once pinpointed the major one when she commented, "You sometimes get more than you bargained for." Earlier in the morning, in preparation for a story about frogs, she had introduced a group of children to a large stuffed frog who was to sit on a chair and listen to them read. The children were delighted. New words in the story were *hop* and *jump.* After they had been written, identified, and discussed, the teacher asked certain children to act out their meanings, which they promptly did with great gusto. Later, after the story had been read, the children were allowed to jump and hop back to their desks, which they again did with obvious enjoyment. The problem? The whole class jumped and hopped for the rest of the morning.

On another day, in another classroom, children had reached the point where they could print their names quite well. They were also able to read a number of words, including *me.* To promote further interest in reading and printing, the teacher typed and dittoed a simple letter that began, "Dear Me." The children each received a copy in a stamped, addressed envelope. What excitement!

A post office was close to the school, so off went the children and the teacher to mail the letters. It was a small office, and arrangements had been made for the children to get a quick tour and an explanation of the facilities.

Upon their return to the classroom, excitement was everywhere. As the teacher observed, "They're really high now." And they were, for the rest of the morning.

Many other examples of the excitability of young children in classrooms could be given. Together, they lead to the same conclusions that could be drawn from the two mentioned:

1. Excitement is easily aroused in young children. It also is contagious.

2. The amount of excitement is not always in proportion to its source. Often, what seems small and unexciting to an adult can create great excitement among young children.

3. The excitement of young children commonly continues after the reason for it is gone. Thus, it is not something that is easily turned off.

4. The great excitability of young children, combined with its tendency to persist, can result in overly stimulated children. It is then that some become undisciplined and rowdy.

5. Taking the characteristics of young children into consideration, teachers should avoid overly stimulating activities.

Imagination

The excitability of young children results from many factors, one of which must surely be their rich imagination. Observations have shown that imagination also brings reality and fantasy very close together, thus allowing young children to be an interesting combination of sophistication and naiveté.

The combination first became noticeable in a kindergarten classroom occupied by what I always thought were unusually sophisticated five-year-olds. They were highly verbal, learned easily, and were surprisingly aware of what was going on in the world. One day, after they had sung and enjoyed a song about a jack-in-the-box, their teacher suggested that each become one. Without hesitation, all these "sophisticates" did just that, hiding their heads in nonexistent boxes. The teacher then said she saw nothing but boxes in her classroom and asked, "But where are the children?" Of course, the "lost" children were delighted and tried all the harder to curl up in their boxes. And the harder they tried, the more I thought, "Such an interesting combination of sophistication and simplicity."

That thought became increasingly common as I visited more and more classrooms. With a first-grade group, for instance, a teacher was using a bulletin-board display to review words the children were learning to read. At the bottom, the board showed an airport. Over it were clouds, and attached to them were small word cards. With this display, children took turns "flying." Using a small paper airplane as a pointer, they pretended to fly up and down in a variety of directions, touching cards and naming words as they flew.

To create interest in what was to be done, the teacher had first talked to the children about the trip they were going to take to the airport and the opportunity they would have to be pilots. And then the flying—and vocabulary review—began.

From the comments the children were making, it appeared that some thought a trip to a real airport was in their future. That this was true of at least two of them was verified later. The teacher received phone calls that evening from two mothers who wondered when the trip to the airport was to be, and how much it would cost. Before the teacher could explain, one even volunteered to go along.

At another time, in a semi-rural nursery school, I had the chance to observe a teacher create interest in numeral identification with the help of a stuffed cloth hen and a group of imaginative four-year-olds. The hen had been placed on a pile of straw; under her were egg-shaped pieces of paper on which numerals from 1 to 10 had been printed. As the teacher took out the eggs one by one, the children named the numerals. After each was correctly identified, it was thumbtacked to the board. All the eggs were counted. Then the children named the numerals again as the teacher took down all but three. The three eggs remaining on the board displayed 3, 5, and 8.

Next came a writing lesson. The numerals 3, 5, and 8 had been selected for additional practice because most of the children had difficulty forming them correctly. As the children began to print, they made a considerable amount of noise because, of course, they still had much to say about the hen. Quickly but kindly the teacher reminded them that the hen was tired from laying so many eggs and needed to rest. No further disturbances occurred as the children proceeded with their work in what was an amazingly quiet room—considering it was filled with four-year-olds who had a hen in their midst.

Many other examples of young children who had imagination and enjoyed using it could be given. Once, a group of children were restless when the teacher wanted them to listen to some directions. Their hands seemed especially busy. Instead of making the more usual request that they fold their hands, the teacher suggested that they be trains and that they hook their hands together the way they had seen train cars being attached. The willingness of the children to do this was immediate and lasted long enough for the teacher to finish the directions.

In another classroom, trains had also been discussed. Later, as the teacher collected pictures of trains drawn by the children, she told them she was a conductor and was collecting tickets. The children loved the idea. Still later, a little girl who always seemed to have trouble sitting for more than two minutes stood up. Instead of chastising her the teacher suggested, "Oh, you had better not stand up. The train might start and then you'd fall and hurt yourself." Very agreeably, the child sat down.

In cases like these, one might ask, Who has the greater imagination—the teacher or the children? In others, the children do the imagining quite on their own. Here I am recalling the number of times parents have told how their young children play school when they get home. (Their imagination freely allows them to use dolls as students.) Once the teaching begins, however, imitation rather than imagination takes over. According to the parents, both the words and the gestures of the teacher at school are imitated by the children with perfection.

Imitation

The tendency of young children to imitate is well known, so I was hardly surprised to find them copying the behavior of others when I visited classrooms. With some, the tendency seemed almost like a compulsion. I recall a variety of children (usually the less mature in a group) who, at least on certain days, copied everything they saw and heard. If the child next to them looked at a picture displayed on a board, they looked at it. If he accidentally fell off his chair, they fell off theirs. With the majority of children, however, imitative behavior was less frequent and seemed normal. For example, to see one child blowing bubbles while drinking milk with a straw and then to see all the others do the same thing seemed very natural indeed.

Fortunately, young children copy the good as well as the bad. I remember one incident in which a first-grade girl suddenly discovered that the color of each of her crayons was printed on its label. With great enthusiasm she began to copy each word with the appropriate color, a somewhat awkward task, since the crayon being used was the one from which the copying had to be done. But she persisted, printing *red* in red, *blue* in blue, and so on. Meanwhile, a classmate came along and asked what she was doing. It wasn't long before the second child was busy with the same task. She wasn't nearly so successful, however. Her first carefully printed word in purple was *crayola*.

In another classroom I saw imitative behavior spread throughout the entire group. These first-graders were busy drawing a picture of a dog like the one in a story that had just been read to them. Before they started, the teacher had labeled each paper with the word *dog* at the bottom. When one of the boys finished his picture, he added what looked like a circle close to the dog's foot. He asked the teacher, "Will you write *food* here?" Soon, food and the second label were being added to everyone's picture.

Suggestibility

Similar to imitative behavior is what might be called the suggestibility of young children. I mention this trait because over and over again while visiting schools, I have been reminded of how easily they are influenced by suggestion. At story-time, for instance, with all the children sitting on the floor in front of her, a teacher might comment, "Can you all see?" Suddenly, once contented children say they cannot see and must move about. Or, as I heard in a kindergarten class, the teacher says, "John, I don't think you can see the pictures from where you're sitting."

Predictably, *all the children* decide they cannot see them and so, once again, everybody must move. Or, to cite another example, because the teacher allows one child to examine a picture in detail, all the children demand to look at it.

In a nursery school, I once watched as a teacher distributed numeral cards to each child in a group of four-year-olds. As she did so, she warned, "Now I don't want any of you to put these cards in your mouth." Very quickly cards were in mouths.

On another day I watched first-graders finishing a writing paper. One child had completed his, so the teacher suggested, "Jeffrey, as long as you're finished you can stand by the door." (It was almost time for outdoor recess.) Suddenly, children who had seemed intent on being careful and correct changed into children who hastily scribbled the last few words on their papers and then eagerly asked, "Can I get in line, too?"

Some of the problems connected with suggestibility are initiated by children. One child says he's cold and needs to get his sweater. Quickly, others who have sweaters need to get them. Or one child gets a paper tissue to blow his nose, and, predictably, several children suddenly have colds and need to go to the tissue box. Or, on another day, one child declares she doesn't like white milk and then many say they don't like white milk.

Fortunately, this great power of suggestion also works for the good. A teacher participates in a word game with a group of children and says for all to hear, "I'm going to listen carefully so that I'll be ready when it's my turn." As a result, at least some in the group listen a little more attentively than they might have done. Or a teacher says to a child, "I certainly like the way you put that *e* on the line," and then many *e*'s are very carefully placed on lines.

What also led to *e*'s on lines, of course, was the praise the children received. Like all other humans, young children respond positively and openly to praise, sometimes adding a little of their own. Here I especially have in mind a little girl who, after being complimented by her teacher for offering a suitable suggestion, said, "That was good head thinking, wasn't it?"

Impatience

What is *not* relished by young children is the need to wait. Yet, in classrooms occupied by large numbers of them and only one adult, waiting is the rule rather than the exception. Waiting to have a turn, for instance, is very common in school. And in this case practice does not make perfect. Repeatedly, I have watched children become inattentive and get into trouble because they were unwilling, or perhaps unable, to be patient and wait their turn.

A behavior problem connected with waiting developed in a first-grade class as the teacher was working with a group of about ten children. Each had been given a number of word cards, and the teacher was building sentences by naming the words. Thus, she might say "the" and the child holding *the* would bring it to a card holder hanging in front of the group, where he would tuck it into a slot. All went well, as long as a child was having a turn. When he was not, especially when all his cards were gone, restlessness and inattentiveness resulted. (Had the teacher been the one who placed the cards as they were brought to her, the routine would have moved along more quickly, and the children would have had more turns faster. In addition, more words and sentences could have been read.)

In still another first grade, the teacher was also working with a group of about ten. In this case she was combining writing and phonics. She would name a word, then choose one child to write its initial letter on the chalkboard. For the child doing the writing, life was great. For all the others, however, it was dull. Why? For one thing, the selected child often took a long time to write a letter; for another, his "audience" was unable to watch as he wrote because he was standing in the way. Eventually, as might be expected, more and more children lost interest, and soon there were discipline problems.

Although taking turns requires an amount of patience that young (and older) children do not always have, once the process is begun, no one is willing to have his turn skipped. One kindergarten teacher, taking advantage of concern about getting a turn, introduced and used alphabetical order. The practice in her classroom was to have a child hold the flag each morning while the others said the pledge of allegiance; turns for this were assigned in alphabetical order. To help, a large alphabetical list of the children's first names was discussed and then displayed low enough for all to see. Never did a child not know when it was his turn to be the flag holder.

Later on, when the children's eagerness to be first in line began to cause problems, the teacher assigned turns using another alphabetical list, this one comprising the children's last names. Predictably, the teacher never once had to ask, "Whose turn is it to be first in line today?"

Sporadically, when difficulties arose because several children wanted to do or use the same thing at the same time, it was common to hear one of them comment, "Let's take alphabet turns." Equally common were objections from children whose names might be Tommy or Vicky or, perhaps, Wilson or Zimmerman. Clearly, the concept of alphabetical order had been learned well.

Misuse of Words

What is not always learned well by young children is the meanings of words. At a time when television-educated children are occupying our classrooms, it is important for teachers to be reminded of this. Otherwise they will assume that more is known than is really the case.

I stress this point because during classroom visits I learned that children who at first seemed highly sophisticated turned out to have many misconceptions. They became apparent most quickly during unstructured conversations. In one, children were talking about the occupations of their fathers. A teaching assistant guided, but did not force, the discussion. At one point a child mentioned that his father was a carpenter, so the assistant asked, "Does everyone know what a carpenter is?" Eagerly one girl volunteered, "I know. He brings your carpet." During the same conversation the discussion turned to occupations the children themselves would like to have when they grew up. The usual ones were mentioned: police officer, cowboy, nurse, mother, and so on. One boy's choice, though, was unexpected. He said that he was going to be an angel because he liked the wings.

During another conversation, which occurred on a Monday morning, children were telling what they had done on Sunday. One girl mentioned that her parents had taken her little brother to church to be advertised. Nobody objected. Apparently, to that group of five-year-olds an advertised baby was as acceptable as one who had been baptized. (For adults, the message might be, "Speak more clearly, please.")

Monday morning in another school revealed that it had been broken into over the weekend. Explaining why the classroom was in such disarray, one first-grade teacher used words that included "vandal" and "vandalism." Later, when I asked one of the boys if he knew who might have done the damage, he replied, "His name is Mr. Vandal."

Misconceptions related to numbers and age also turned out to be common. In one classroom, a teacher was discussing the approaching presidential election and explained that a person had to be twenty-one years old to vote. "Twenty-one!" exclaimed a boy. "If you were twenty-one you'd be a grandpa."* In a kindergarten that I visited regularly, misconceptions about age came closer to home when a girl said to me, "You're just a kid, aren't you?" Delighted—but curious— I asked why she thought I was a kid. Her explanation? "You don't wear buttons on your ears."

Self-Awareness

While interesting misconceptions were revealed by children, the same individuals also displayed a surprising amount of astuteness regarding themselves and their abilities. I can recall a four-year-old who had been taught to print his name and who, for the first time, was looking at a typed version of it. His reaction? "That looks gooder than the way I make it." While cutting out the outline of a house, another four-year-old observed, "I'm having trouble steering." In a kindergarten, one little girl looked at the S she had just printed and complained, "I can't make S. Up here it's bigger and down there it's littler." As he watched a group of children print numerals on the chalkboard, a kindergarten boy in another school was heard to say, "I make good 5's now. I used to make messy ones."

Awareness of their ability in reading was noted in still other children. Quite on her own a girl lamented, "I'm having trouble with *house* and *horse*. Is that

---

* This conversation took place before the age requirement was changed to eighteen years. For the child in question, however, it is likely that an eighteen-year-old was ancient, too.

house or *horse?*" Another was observed reading to several other children from a book that included some pages with pictures and very few words and some pages with nothing but words. Because of her limited ability, she did fine with the first type but seemed to know she had met her Waterloo each time she came to the second. But she found a solution. Whenever she came to the more densely worded pages she simply explained, "Oh, I don't like this. I don't think I'll read it."

Other kinds of awareness also became apparent during visits to classrooms, some of which—I must admit—surprised me. In one nursery school class a teacher had dittoed pictures of a telephone that were to be used for practice in printing phone numbers. Approximately one second after a boy received his copy he objected, "That's wrong. The zero should have the word *operator* next to it."

In another nursery school, a four-year-old had been coughing. As soon as she was able to catch her breath she said—and with considerable disappointment in her voice—"I don't even smoke and I still have a bad cough."

How television has invaded the lives and thoughts of young children became apparent many other times, but never so strikingly as in one conversation between a kindergartner and his teacher. Like the others in his class, this boy had been practicing making a *d,* but he was forming it incorrectly. When the teacher stopped at his desk and noticed this, she commented about it and then showed him the correct form. A child who always had to get in the last word, he said to her, "I like to do it my own way." Patiently the teacher explained that in school he was supposed to learn how to do things the right way, which might not always be his way. Unwilling to go down in defeat, the five-year-old proceeded to tell about the campus fights he had seen on television, pointing out that people sometimes learn to do the wrong things in school.

Fortunately, other instances of young children's awareness seemed more childlike. Complaints about books (for example, "The story says the top is red, but the picture makes it look orange," or "Kittens don't say 'mew mew.' They say 'mow, mow,'") were easy to accept. So, too, was the comment of a girl who, when her teacher spoke softly, was quick to say, "Mrs. T——, you sound so weak!" And the comment of a boy cannot be bypassed. When he arrived at school one morning, he looked at the teacher and immediately observed, "I bet you put curlers in your hair last night. That's how come you've got curls on the top of your head."

Independence

Although dependence is part of the very essence of childhood, it is still true to say that the more young children learn to do, the more they want to do on their own. In so many ways this move toward independence was seen in classroom behavior. Even among five-year-olds who were just learning to print their names, it was not uncommon to find some who refused to use models (small name cards) made by the teacher because, they explained, "I know how to do it." After many classroom visits I was hardly surprised to hear a first-grader complain because the teacher was labeling objects in her picture. "Why can't we do that our own selves?" was the way she phrased her disappointment. And even four-year-olds are not about to accept help when it is unnecessary. One time, a nursery school teacher was calling the children's attention to the names of certain numerals. She did this by writing and then naming them, frequently asking the children to watch. In response, one boy said with pride rather than boldness, "I don't have to look because I know what it looks like."

Art projects also revealed the growing independence of young children. Once, a nursery school class was asked to draw pictures of a dog who had been described earlier in a story. He was brown and white, and it was presumed that the children would make their pictures the same colors. However, one boy informed the teacher that he was going to make his "a rainbow dog." She explained that the dog was to be the one in the story, so he had to be colored brown and white. The boy seemed resigned. Later, when he brought his picture to the teacher, the dog *was* brown and white—but he was wearing a rainbow-colored sweater.

On another occasion, this time in a kindergarten, children were making pictures of Indians. One mentioned that Indians never wore clothes, so he wasn't going to put any on his. The idea spread and was quickly accepted by the others. Probably concerned about what parents might think when their children brought home pictures of naked people, the teacher said rather firmly that Indians *did* wear clothes. The children, nonetheless, were not about to change their minds. Sensing this, the teacher left the visitor "in charge" and departed. A few minutes later she returned with a library book that included many colorful pictures of Indians wearing clothes. She showed the children the pictures; she also reminded them that it was chilly outside and they must not let their Indians catch cold. The last point seemed to be taken quite seriously by the children, for they proceeded to dress their Indians.

Enjoyment of Challenges

Another characteristic of young children as they learn is their enjoyment of a challenge. All a teacher has to say is, "I bet I can fool you," and suddenly all eyes and ears are working. Should a teacher's error be observed, even more delighted children are the result. With this in mind, a first-grade teacher was able to add interest to a review of the written names of colors simply by saying, "I'm not sure I can remember all these words. I'll try to read them, but tell me if I make a mistake." Predictably, all watched intently and then were obviously pleased to catch and correct the teacher's "errors."

Of course, teachers' errors are not always deliberate. I recall a kindergarten discussion of a very attractive display of Halloween pictures, each coupled with a simple label. At the time, the teacher was using the display for practice in counting, so things like pumpkins, ghosts, and bats were being counted by the children. Reaching a picture that was labeled *3 bats,* the teacher asked, "How many bats are on the board?" Almost in unison the children eagerly informed her that the label was wrong because there were four bats. And there were. One appeared in another picture and was almost made invisible because of its small size. A child in the group probably expressed the feelings of all when she said to the teacher, "I liked it when we caught you."

Nonpredictability

It is possible that an erroneous conclusion might be drawn from this discussion of the characteristics of young children; namely, that their behavior is always predictable. Actually, as any parent or experienced teacher will verify, it is not. For example, what we know about children suggests that if four-year-olds are taken to a hatchery, they will be willing and even eager to discuss what they saw the next morning. Yet I was in a nursery school classroom the morning following just such a trip and heard one boy object as the group began to discuss it. "How come we're still talking about chickens?" was his complaint.

Probably, unexpected behavior occurs most frequently when a school program for young children has academic goals, because academic accomplishments make the children seem older than their age. As a result, when they display behavior that reflects actual age, it is surprising. I recall one kindergarten girl who burst into tears when the teacher unintentionally passed her by as she was distributing little rhythm band instruments during music. Such a response seemed so out of character because the weeping child was one who learned everything that was ever taught—or merely mentioned. Consequently, she did seem "too big" to cry about some triviality, but cry she did.

An able girl in another kindergarten also took everyone by surprise with her tears. At the time, the children were printing each letter in their last names on small square pieces of paper. Eventually, the squares were to be pasted in correct sequence on a large sheet of paper. This particular girl, as would be expected, had no trouble with the printing or with arranging the letters in order. However, when she went to paste her unusually long name on the paper, it didn't fit. And then came the tears.

Other unexpected behavior often shows up as young children respond to "lessons." I remember one teacher—always a careful planner—who used an interesting collection of colored pictures to introduce a discussion of clouds. Later, the children were to be taken outdoors to look at some, but at the start, they examined and discussed the pictures. After arousing the children's curiosity, the teacher read from a book that told some interesting facts about cloud formations. As I watched, the children listened attentively and seemed interested. Then, just before they were to go outside, the teacher held up a picture that showed stars in addition to the clouds. One child's immediate and excited response? "Oh, it's the Fourth of July." And soon everyone was talking at once about fireworks and sparklers. Gone was the carefully nourished interest in clouds.

Even with games, children react in unexpected ways. I first learned this while watching a group of children play Musical Chairs. Inclement weather had made indoor recess necessary, so the teacher lined up chairs and the game began. But then problems developed when everyone wanted to be a loser. Why a loser? Because in some unplanned way the loser got to carry away a chair, and that was very special for a reason not at all obvious to the two adults who watched.

Probably the underlying lesson to be learned from all these accounts of the behavior of young children can be summed up with a simple prediction directed to their teachers: *Never* will there be a dull moment in a classroom filled with four-, five-, and six-year-old children.

REVIEW

1. *Nonpredictability* was identified in Chapter 1 as one characteristic of young children. Is there an inherent contradiction in the claims that (a) certain behavior is characteristic, and (b) nonpredictability *is* one of the characteristics?

2. Chapter 1 discussed young children's attention spans, which is an important topic because attention and achievement go hand-in-hand. Because it *is* important, let me mention what I once observed in a kindergarten. The teacher was having the children take turns spelling their first names. With so many in the group, this took a long time. It also created very restless children. Later, when I asked about the reason for such a procedure, the teacher explained, "Doing something like that with an entire class encourages lengthy attention spans." Do you agree?

3. All teachers are concerned about discipline problems. Since they are, it is surprising to find that some unintentionally create problems themselves. Chapter 1 referred to four procedures that prompt misbehavior. List them. (We'll return to your list following Chapter 2.)

4. The explicit intent of Chapter 1 was to discuss children's characteristic behavior. Nonetheless, a number of references were made to instruction and practice. Can you recall examples of both that would be highly desirable (productive and of interest) with younger children?

5. In the Preview of Chapter 1, you were encouraged to compare what you know about young children with what was reported in the chapter. Having done that, what are your conclusions? Does the chapter describe the children you know? What characteristics would you either eliminate from, or add to, the account presented in Chapter 1?

CHAPTER

2

Classroom Behavior of Teachers of Young Children

PREVIEW

Although the teachers depicted in Chapter 2 were with young children when they were observed, the lessons to be learned from their behavior and that of the children have broad significance. I myself became aware of this the hard way.

To illustrate, the chapter reminds teachers about the importance of distributing materials at the right time—not too early and not too late. The chapter especially notes that premature distribution encourages young children to play with the materials when they should be listening to directions for using them.

Since I wrote Chapter 2, one would think I'd remember its warning. Evidently I forgot it one evening when one of my graduate classes was just getting underway. Knowing that I had an unusually large number of things to cover in the two-hour period, I made the mistake of immediately distributing all the handouts (to save time), each of which would be referred to at various times during class. The result? The handouts were major distractions for about the first fifteen minutes, and minor ones for the rest of the two hours.

The point is that much of what is said in Chapter 2 is relevant for more than teachers of the young.

As Chapter 2 tells about the behavior of teachers, it also refers to instruction and practice. Don't forget all this as you go through the chapter.

A picture of the successful teacher has gradually evolved for me as a result of observing in numerous classrooms, many of them visited at regular intervals. It is possible, of course, that some of the pieces composing it were selected for subjective reasons. Yet, even if the pieces do suffer from all the limitations of subjectivity, the total picture can still make a contribution if it prompts you to think more carefully about your own teaching or about your current conception of what the "good" teacher is and does. The possibility of this occurring is, I believe, reason enough to discuss what might only be personal, nonscientific conclusions.

My own conception of the successful teacher of young children began to develop as I watched not the teachers but, rather, the children. When I saw children who appeared to be pleased and happy about attending school, I assumed their teachers must be doing something right. When I had the chance to observe children who were not only content but also busy and involved with school activities, then it seemed even more likely that they had "good" teachers. And when I saw children who liked school and wanted to come; who were interested in, and involved with, what was going on; and, who were learning what had been planned for them to learn and even more, I was convinced that their teachers merited such laudatory descriptions as "successful" and "effective."

PROBLEMS WITH SPECIFIC DESCRIPTIONS

What were these teachers like? Before answering, let me first warn about a problem that can develop whenever the specifics of instruction are made visible—whether in a demonstration or on television or, for instance, through the silent language of the written page.

The problem I refer to is the tendency—particularly prevalent among those who are preparing for teaching—to want to imitate specifically described behavior. It is a problem because effective instruction is never just a matter of copying what a successful teacher is doing. This statement is true for a variety of reasons. One is that what turns out to be successful teaching with one group of children will not necessarily be successful with another. A second reason is that while it is somewhat possible to copy what another teacher does and says, it is never possible to copy what she or he is. This distinction is an especially important one, for it recognizes that every teacher is a person as well as an instructor and that both roles are important in determining what will constitute successful teaching *for that teacher.*

For me, the key role played by the personality of a teacher has been highlighted whenever I have combined teacher education with classroom observations. I recall working very closely with two teachers whose personalities could not have been more diverse. What remains particularly vivid about the experience is how differently the two put the very same suggestions into practice. I could feel nothing but pride as I observed the first using an idea or a procedure that I had recommended in a conference. Yet, when I visited the second teacher —and she had attended the same conference—I felt some chagrin that I might have contributed to what she was doing.

At another time, I was trying to help just one teacher. In this case, tremendous amounts of help were required because for many years her first-grade program had been characterized by unchanging routines, a paucity of materials, and many rules about talking, raising hands, keeping a straight line, and so on. My most vivid and lasting recollection is the way this teacher used a recommendation to turn at least some word-identification practice into games. The recommendation had been bolstered by many specific ideas that other teachers had used successfully; thus, hope for success in this classroom did not seem unrealistic.

When I next visited, the teacher was using one of the suggestions. She began by announcing to the group of children with whom she was working, "I want absolute silence because you've got to learn to play a game today." Following the wholly unexpected introduction, she proceeded to lay down the various rules and regulations. Finally, the game began. At the end, all the children were holding word cards they had identified correctly; therefore, as would be expected of any young children who could count, they started to count their cards aloud to see who had the most. Immediately the teacher said, "This is not a game for counting. I want that talking stopped."

I had two reactions: This is a game? Am I the cause of this? More lasting reactions have been a clearer recognition of the important role played by personality and the uselessness of imitating the behavior of a successful teacher as a way of becoming one.

With these observations in the background, it should now be clear that the descriptions of successful teachers to be presented in this chapter are not meant to foster imitation. Instead, they are included with the hope that making the act of teaching visible and specific will help those who have not yet taught. For those of you who are teaching, the descriptions may offer suggestions that you can incorporate into your work *in your own way*. The descriptions will also demonstrate a few standards against which you may want to evaluate some of your current procedures and practices.

CHARACTERISTICS OF SUCCESSFUL TEACHERS

What becomes apparent most quickly whenever successful teachers are observed is that they work hard. To be sure, experience does reduce the amount of work required. Still, in all classrooms in which I had the privilege of observing good

teachers, it was very clear that what they did and were able to accomplish resulted from much work and careful planning. This observation underscores the
fact that successful instruction is not an accident. Or, to make the same point
positively, good teachers work for their success.

Other qualities also characterize good teachers. They are described below.

Ability to Take into Account the Characteristics of Young Children

The importance of taking young children's characteristics into account has been
highlighted as much by poor as by successful teachers.* One characteristic, for
example, is the tendency to turn everything into a toy and, therefore, to see everything as something to play with. It is not surprising, therefore, that when materials like pencil and paper are distributed *before* directions for using them are
given, the children will play with them—perhaps even scribble—*while* the teacher
gives the directions. The inevitable results are misused materials, unheard directions, and wasted time.

Another observable characteristic of young children is the ease with which
they can be distracted. Call it lack of self-discipline, inability to resist temptation,
or immaturity. The label is unimportant. The simple fact is that young children
can easily be distracted; therefore, teachers should take this into account when
working with them. Do they?

I recall being in one first grade when the teacher was working with six children. She was printing words on a chalkboard; the children were sitting in front
of the board and were expected to be looking at the words and identifying them.
There was a problem, however. Next to the board was a small, low table. On it
were clay figures of animals that the children had made the day before. *Naturally,*
they were an attraction, even though they had been discussed the day before.
Naturally, two children in the group of six were more interested in looking at the
animals than at the words on the board. Instead of taking this very normal response into account and dealing with it (this could have been done by simply
moving the table to another part of the room), the teacher scolded the children
for not paying attention. The final results were much wasted time and, as might
be expected, two children who still gave more attention to clay animals than to
words on a chalkboard.

How a highly effective first-grade teacher handled a similar situation merits
a description. This teacher had given two written assignments to a group of children with whom she had just finished working. One of the assignments made use
of Indian headbands that had been made earlier in the week. It required the chil-

---

* References to less than excellent teachers are not intended to be criticisms. Rather,
they reflect the fact that it is often easier to learn about the requirements of success by watching the obviously unsuccessful person. Effective teachers, I learned, typically go about their
work with such ease that they encourage an observer to erroneously conclude that what they
are doing is easy.

dren to select from a page of small pictures those whose names began with the short sound of *i,* to cut them out, and to paste them on the headbands as a decoration. As soon as the headbands were distributed the group became excited and noisy, apparently forgetting the other work that was to be done. Aware of her mistake in passing out the headbands too soon, the teacher wisely bypassed chastisement and said instead, "I don't think you'll have enough room on your desks for the headbands. Maybe it would be a good idea to put them back on the table until you finish the two workbook pages. When I check them and find that all your answers are correct, you can put the workbooks away and then there will be plenty of room to do a good job with the headbands." No child objected, and the practice period proceeded without further disruptions.

How people deal with behavior that is disruptive has a great deal to do with whether or not they will be successful as teachers. Those who *are* successful have learned to deal with it in ways that are both effective and acceptable to the children. Thus, the teacher who, instead of ordering a child to put an annoying trinket away, simply suggests, "It might be a good idea to put that in your pocket; otherwise you'll lose it," will have a more positive relationship with the child and a better chance of changing his behavior. With something like writing practice, the successful teacher of young children avoids negative and discouraging comments and in their place makes observations like, "Oh, that *t* got in too much hot water and shrank. You'll have to make it bigger." When numerals are being practiced, she might say to a child who is having problems, "That five is a shorty. He needs to grow taller so that he'll be as big as the other numerals. You don't want him to be sad, do you?"

A somewhat dramatic example of how another successful teacher dealt with undesirable behavior occurred in a kindergarten. In this case, a boy displayed a boldness that startled everyone—including, I thought, the boy himself. For a brief moment, his behavior brought total silence to the room. Then, with great poise, the teacher calmly looked at him and started to sing—with just the right amount of sternness—a song called, "Watch What that Little Tongue Says." Within a short time, everything was back to normal.

On another occasion, the same teacher quieted a group of children who were all talking at once with another song, "Only One Can Talk at a Time." She also turned out to be a teacher who, rather than ordering a group to listen and pay attention, was apt to say something like, "I'm looking for closed doors [mouths] and open windows [eyes]."

What was always apparent, and even striking, about the way this particular teacher dealt with undesirable behavior was that her methods were both effective *and* acceptable to the children. It seems she not only knew and took into account their characteristics but also enjoyed them.

Teachers' acceptance of the normal characteristics of the age group with which they work is important for professional satisfaction. The behavior of teachers in a few classrooms that were visited regularly suggested that they might have been happier working with older students. For instance, one teacher commonly scolded children for doing things such as stamping their feet when a child in the story being read stamped his, or asking, "Where's the cowboys?" after she read, "They played Indians." In another classroom, a teacher became quite perturbed with a child because, just briefly, he pretended his paste bottle was binoculars and proceeded to examine objects scattered about the room. This same teacher also tended to argue with children:

Teacher: These are new books.

Child: I've seen them before.

Teacher: No, you have not.

Child: My brother had them.

Teacher: I said these are new books.

Personally, I have always thought that one of the most appealing characteristics of young children is their unexpected answers; consequently, the behavior of another frequently observed teacher was surprising because she seemed so unaccepting of anything unusual. Once, for example, she was discussing the color red and asked the children to name red things. At first, ordinary responses like "fire truck" and "traffic light" were given, and they were accepted with a smile. They were also printed on the board so that soon the following list was available:

fire truck

traffic light

wagon

apple

strawberry

After the response of "strawberry," an interesting but disappointing thing occurred. One child eagerly contributed "sore tonsils," but his response was ignored.

On another day, another child received a similar reaction to his unexpected answer. He was in a group that was reading a story about bakers, who were pictured as being clothed entirely in white. "Why do you suppose bakers wear white clothing?" was one of the questions posed by the teacher. As the children proceeded to offer explanations, it became clear that the teacher wanted them to refer to the need to be clean when working with food. One boy, ignoring the hints, explained, "If the baker drops flour on his clothes, nobody will know they're dirty." Again, the answer received no response.

Fortunately, visits to most classrooms occupied by young children provide opportunities to watch teachers who seem not only to understand their particular characteristics but also to enjoy them. Thus, I have seen teachers who:

- Prepared a trayful of small objects and trinkets whose names began with *t* as a way of helping children enjoy phonics instruction.

- Used a puppet to make counting more interesting.

- Promised the children a rectangle surprise when they were talking about rectangles and later carried in four small, rectangular chalkboards, to the delight of the children.

- Prepared for use in Monday morning's phonics instruction a bulletin-board display portraying a Saturday night television program called "The Mouse on the Mayflower."

Sensitivity to Individual Needs and Problems

Successful teachers, as has been emphasized, are knowledgeable about young children and enjoy them—at least most of the time. A related characteristic is their sensitivity to the needs and problems of individual children.

I became consciously aware of this trait early in my observations. Its importance was initially made clear in a kindergarten in which there was an exceedingly bright girl—in fact, she was one of the brightest young children I have known. Yet, for reasons I do not pretend to understand, she became tense and anxious whenever she was asked to do something alone. It could be as simple as reading a word or pointing to a particular picture. The nature of the task did not matter, nor did her outstanding ability and accomplishments. She simply could not cope with situations that called attention to herself. Luckily, she was with a teacher who quickly sensed the problem and went out of her way to avoid placing the child in any situation that called for a solo performance. Eventually, but very slowly, this girl was able to overcome the problem, although at the end of the year she still was not one who went out of her way to "perform."

What on the surface also looked like excessive shyness appeared in a boy in another kindergarten. To him, having to do anything physical seemed like an unbearable burden. During music, for instance, when the other children were merrily skipping or, perhaps, dramatizing the words of a song, he acted as if his greatest desire was to find a hole and hide. Sensitive to the problem, his teacher never commented about it and said nothing when he chose to remain apart from an activity. Occasionally she offered encouragement, but nothing more. Again, little by little, this child was able to join the others—although with great hesitation at first.

Other combinations of sensitive teachers and children with problems were found in many other classrooms. In a first-grade group, one girl seemed unusually intimidated by children who knew more than she did. The teacher took cognizance of this when she organized instructional groups, always placing her in one in which she was likely to know either as much as, or more than, the other children. Such careful placement seemed to bolster the child's self-confidence; at least, by the end of the year she was not so readily squelched by children who knew more than she did.

Whole groups of children also benefited from sensitive teachers. This became especially noticeable on days when restlessness pervaded an entire class. On such days, these teachers allotted a longer amount of time for recess and, for example, planned a music period in which the children not only sang but also marched, skipped, jumped, and hopped. As one of these teachers noted, "On a day like this, I always make sure there's plenty of wiggle music."

Common Sense

In addition to being sensitive to the needs and problems of individual children, successful teachers also make abundant use of common sense. Admittedly, "common sense" is neither an informative nor a scholarly description; yet I hardly know how else to categorize the requirements for success that I identified indirectly by watching poor rather than good teachers. Therefore, let me describe certain behaviors of the former; then you can assign your own descriptive heading to this section of the chapter.

One common behavior was the failure to make sure that children were able to see what was going on. To describe how this lack of attention to a very important detail was revealed, let me reproduce below a few of the notes I made following observations. In all instances, teachers' names have been changed.

- In her work with small groups today, Mrs. Graves used a large chart on which words had been printed. The chart was hung so low that most of the children were unable to see the words at the bottom.

- Today Miss Hutchins played a game with small groups of children as a way of providing word practice. A group divided into two teams whose members lined up on opposite sides of the room. The game proceeded by having team members take turns identifying words shown on cards held by Miss Hutchins. Unfortunately, she held up each card in such a way that only the members of the team whose turn it was could see it. This reduced by half the amount of practice that could have been possible.

- Each reading group in Miss Marlan's class is made up of about eight children who sit in one row of chairs at the front of the room. This morning, instruction for each group began with a review that had individual children identify words printed on cards held by Miss Marlan. Because of the length of the row of chairs, children sitting at one end were unable to see words being identified by children at the other end.

- Today, some of the tiniest children in Mrs. Ray's room ended up sitting in the second of the two rows of chairs used when small-group instruction takes place. This created obvious problems whenever Mrs. Ray wrote words on the chalkboard; still, no effort was made to have the shorter children sit in the front row.

- Today Mrs. Wonder had children identify words as they framed them. (The words were printed on the chalkboard.) To do this, they had to stand in front of the word, thus preventing others from seeing it as it was being identified. One further problem was a table that was next to the chalkboard. Its presence required the children to lean across it, resulting in much stumbling and giggling but little practice.

Additional notes further emphasized the necessity of attending to small but important details:

- Today, when Mrs. Green placed word cards in the slots in the card holder, the bottoms of the cards in one row were commonly covered by the cards placed in the next row. This created problems whenever the covered words included letters with descenders. Partially covered, g looked like a manuscript a, while y looked like v.

- As Miss Ninsley holds up word cards, her fingers frequently cover the bottoms of letters with descenders. Sometimes that is enough to give a word a distorted appearance.

- Today, Mrs. Winters had a number of word cards that she showed to the children one at a time. All the cards were the same size, except for a longer one on which she had printed *something*. This created two problems. First, the unusual length of the one card could be used as a cue in identifying *something*. Second, because all the cards were being held together, the *ing* in *something* extended out from the rest. This meant that as each word was shown to the children, they saw that word plus *ing* at the end of it.

Other notes raised questions about teacher-made materials. For instance, one practice sheet showed a list of ten typed sentences. The job for the children was to read each and underline the one word that contained a short *o* sound. The surprising feature of the sheet was that all the words to be underlined appeared at the ends of the sentences. Also a cause for surprise were other dittoed assignment sheets in which letters were either not printed clearly or not printed at all. Such imperfections always caused problems for the children; yet they appeared repeatedly.

In some of the schools that were visited, teachers gave a great deal of time to preparing interesting materials, which was encouraging. But some of the materials contained flaws that were so obvious they were also surprising. One hard-working teacher, for instance, had taken the time to print words on paper apples. (The apples were to be placed on a bulletin-board tree, if the words were correctly identified.) Unfortunately, the red chosen for the apples was dark; as a result, it was almost impossible to read the words because they had been printed with a black crayon.

Great difficulty in seeing what a teacher had so carefully printed occurred in another classroom, in which the cars of a train, each a different color, were hanging on a wall. The intent was to display various colors and the word for each. Thus, *red* had been printed on the red car, *yellow* on the yellow car, and so on. The obvious problem was that the words were so small they could not be read from where the children sat.

Another teacher had drawn the face of a clock on a paper plate. It was to be used for numeral-identification practice, so numerals from 1 to 12 had been carefully printed around the edge. There also was a movable hand, made from paper and attached to the center of the plate. But there was a problem. The hand was so long it covered the numerals as it pointed to them. This flaw could have been eliminated with the snip of a scissors, but instead—again surprisingly—the teacher used the plate without making the small but important adjustment.

Other surprises underscored the importance of "Be prepared!" A few new teachers habitually demonstrated its importance when they lost the children's attention because they had to look for this and that. Apparently, they had failed to think through the requirements of a particular assignment or type of instruction; the result was the need to get or find something right in the middle of a lesson or an explanation. Predictably, the children lost interest in the job at hand and, commonly, did not regain it when the necessary materials were finally collected.

Failure to think about necessary materials was displayed in other ways, too. One assignment in a first-grade classroom required the children to read color words in order to know what color to make certain objects in a dittoed picture. Not all the children knew every word, so the teacher reminded them that all they had to do was look at a chart in the front of the room if they had trouble. The chart showed rectangles of various colors, each labeled with the appropriate color word. An obvious shortcoming, however, was that the assignment used two words (*purple* and *brown*) that were not included in the chart. As a result, the "independent" assignment turned into an occasion for many questions.

In another classroom, the importance of being prepared was underscored as a teacher worked with a group of about seven children. She commented about having just a small amount of time for review and proceeded to write a sentence on the chalkboard. The children read it, then waited while another sentence was written. (While they waited, they also talked.) Because of the brief amount of time that was available, only four sentences were read. Had the teacher prepared for the review by writing sentences on cards or a chart, many more than just four could have been read in the same amount of time.

All these observations can be summed up by saying that effective instruction is made up of many component parts, one of which is giving attention to small but important details.

Ability to Select Appropriate Instructional Goals

Effective teaching is also marked by appropriate goals. In this context, it is relevant to point out that even though the teaching manuals that come with textbooks *can* be useful, they cannot guarantee that the goals they enumerate are the most appropriate for particular children.

Take a goal like "review vocabulary," for instance. For some children it may be necessary; for others, it is a waste of time. This was displayed in one kindergarten in which the teacher was reviewing words that had been introduced earlier in connection with outdoor signs. She first worked with the lowest achievers. The words were written, identified, and discussed; then a game was played in which the children had to act out the meanings of the words, now appearing on homemade signs. With this group, the goal was appropriate and the means taken to achieve it were effective. At least the children seemed to be both learning from and enjoying the game.

When the same procedures were used later with brighter children, it immediately became clear that they knew the words as well as the teacher; consequently, review hardly seemed necessary. Nonetheless, the teacher went right on, repeating everything that had been done with the others. Now, though, the results were different. In a matter of a few minutes, the children lost interest in the game, probably because it offered no challenge. But still the teacher persisted.

Even when goals *are* appropriate, failure to keep them in mind can get in the way of reaching them in the most efficient way. Exemplifying this fact is a common occurrence in classrooms in which young children are learning about the sounds letters record. To reinforce a certain letter-sound association (goal), teachers often have children underline pictures whose names begin with the selected sound and then, typically, they direct the children to color the pictures. Such an activity might take about twenty minutes, five of which are spent on sounds while the remaining time is consumed with the coloring. Teachers who keep the instructional goal in mind ("Why am I doing what I'm doing?") spend the fifteen minutes helping individual children with the sound. Those who do not are more apt to spend it supervising the coloring.

Because children *will* be children, the point must also be made that even when both goals and the procedures for accomplishing them are appropriate and are kept in mind, things still do not always go as planned. A boy in a kindergarten reminded me of this. He and some other children were playing bingo with the teacher. This game had been selected as a way of reviewing words that were printed on the cards. As in any bingo game, the children received markers; in this case, paper squares. As it happened, the boy referred to above became much more interested in counting and comparing squares than in covering words. And the interest spread to the entire group. Since it became clear from their responses that practice in counting and comparing also were appropriate goals, the teacher wisely switched the focus temporarily. After a while, interest in the words returned, and the bingo game proceeded in the way the teacher had originally planned to play it.

Flexibility

The bingo incident identifies another characteristic that is common among successful teachers. They have definite plans; yet they are flexible and are able to see in a situation a potential not originally thought about or planned for. Call it *flexible structure* or *structured flexibility*. The point is that teachers who are successful are well organized, yet always open to unforeseen possibilities. A few such teachers are described below:

- While teaching the song "B-I-N-G-O," one teacher remembered to print the five letters for all the children to see. This was in keeping with one of the current instructional goals: letter-naming ability.

- A group of children were talking about a recent PTA Carnival during a conversation period, after which the teacher wrote PTA on the board and explained that it was an example of what they had talked about earlier in the week: abbreviations.

- A child observed, "So many begin with *J!*" while attendance was being taken with the help of first-name cards tucked into the slots of a word-card holder. Since the children were learning about letter-sound associations, the teacher correctly took time to print and read the four names that started with *J*.

What occurred in still another classroom should be mentioned, too, because it points up another of the requirements for successful instruction. My purpose in working with this kindergarten teacher was to show that everyday happenings often provide opportunities to expose young children to written words and that, as a result, some children learn to read them. To start, I suggested that whenever words of special interest came up, some might be printed on the board so that the children could see as well as hear them. Apparently, I was unsuccessful in communicating my idea because when I next visited, the teacher wrote practically every word she spoke. The result was a group of children who were being deluged by many words rather than exposed to a few special ones. For me, the result was a new awareness of the importance of, "A little goes a long way."

Ability to Know the Meaning of "Enough"

Once more I am at a loss to know exactly how to label a characteristic—this time, the ability that allows a teacher to appreciate that a little goes a long way; to have a sense of proportion; and to know when it is time to quit. I have called it the ability to know the meaning of *enough*. Descriptions of a few teachers who did too much or went too far should help clarify both the meaning of what I am trying to name and its importance for teaching.

The first teacher who comes to mind was unusually successful in assembling interesting bulletin-board displays that had much instructional potential. The children's enthusiastic response probably was the reason for an unfortunate development. As the school year progressed, one attractive bulletin board was replaced by two. Gradually, the two were replaced by three until, at one point, everything in the room was covered, including the one chalkboard.

Two consequences of this failure to appreciate the importance of "enough" are worth mentioning. One was that the lack of a chalkboard interfered with instruction, at times making it impossible to show what the children needed to see. Another consequence was a room in which the displays were an unsettling distraction rather than an interesting aid. Obviously being demonstrated was that four good bulletin-board displays are not four times as helpful as one. Also shown was the ease with which means can become ends in themselves.

In another classroom, I had suggested that an attempt be made to help the children become more consciously aware of written words in their everyday surroundings, including those appearing on television and in newspapers. In response, the teacher developed a News Bulletin Board. The children were encouraged to bring in known words in newspapers, which were displayed on the board. For about a week, the group's response to news was one of considerable interest and involvement, and they eagerly named letters, read words, and even talked about current events. But then it became obvious that with the passing of each day, this interest waned. And yet the teacher continued to have news time every morning. By the end of about three weeks, it had turned into a time of discipline problems and was finally discontinued. Once again, the meaning of "too much of a good thing" became crystal clear.

It was also made clear in a kindergarten in which there were both a teacher and an aide. The children were learning to name letters and to read some words. Toward the end of the year, as a way of helping with both goals, the teacher used an alphabet record in which the narrator spent considerable time on each letter. This enabled the teacher to write a letter on one chalkboard as the narrator discussed it while, on another, the aide printed a word (a familiar one whenever possible) that began with that letter. To an observer it seemed that the children enjoyed both the record and the extra touches added by the teacher and her assistant. From an instructional point of view, the procedure offered interesting review as well as an opportunity to expose the children to some new words. But then something else was done.

Encouraged by the children's positive response, the teacher later decided to use the same procedure with another record, this one dealing with the months of the year. But there was an important difference, which apparently was overlooked. With the second record, each month was considered only briefly, requiring the teacher to print the letters and the aide the names of the months so quickly that the procedure was anything but instructive. Once more the message that came through was the importance of appropriateness, of knowing when to quit, of sensing what is too much.

For me, one of the most difficult things to communicate to teachers is this sense of knowing what is the right amount. Even when I work closely with individual teachers, communication often breaks down when it comes to this. As a result, things like the following have occurred. I mentioned to one teacher (and we discussed in some detail specific ways for carrying out this suggestion) that children's names are useful in teaching and reviewing the names of letters. A subsequent visit to her classroom showed a procedure in which she was having *every* child, one after the other, spell his name. Since the class was large, the activity lasted much longer than the children's attention.

Knowledgeability

The last characteristic of successful teachers that will be named is knowledgeability. Had this chapter been written at another time, such a requirement probably would have been bypassed, not because it is unimportant but because its importance is so obvious. However, not long ago I overheard a conversation in which someone expressed the opinion, "You don't have to know very much to teach young children." The chapter will therefore conclude with a few comments about the need for teachers of the young to be *very* knowledgeable.

Traditionally, as has been pointed out, individuals and professional groups connected with early childhood education stressed the need for teachers to be knowledgeable about the psychology of young children. Because they considered social and emotional development to be the major goal of school programs, such an emphasis was natural, as was the fact that teacher education programs were heavily weighted with courses in child development.

Now that the child's early years are considered to be uniquely important for intellectual development, other emphases have come to the foreground. Nonetheless, the need to understand and even enjoy the behavior and characteristics of young children continues to be an essential requirement for their teachers. Added to this one, however, is the need to be knowledgeable about subject matter and how it might be taught to the young.

Because agreement about the best subject matter for early childhood programs does not exist, neither does agreement about what teachers must know. The contention of this book is that the language arts comprise the most important foci for instruction; consequently, its chapters deal with content designed to help teachers know what is necessary for teaching skills concerned with listening, speaking, reading, and writing.

What is necessary, incidentally, is much more than what will actually be taught because successful teaching requires an amount of knowledge that allows for selection of content that is appropriate for particular children. And this brings the discussion right back to individualized instruction. Individualized instruction, you will recall, is any instruction that corresponds to what children need and are ready to learn. While it is a lofty goal, it is not an unattainable one.

Because a maximum of individualized instruction is the aim of this book, the chapters do not prescribe what *must* be taught to all children attending nursery school, kindergarten, or first grade. Clearly, any such prescriptions go contrary to the very essence of individualized instruction. Instead, the chapters consider language arts content in a way that should allow teachers to select from it whatever seems appropriate for the children who are their responsibility. Because one selection must be followed by another, the chapters also consider sequence by pointing out what tends to be easier and more simple than something else. Like the present chapter, those dealing with the content of instruction try to make the act of teaching as specific as possible.

REVIEW

1. In some ways, Chapter 2 comes close to suggesting that superior teachers are born, not made. What's your opinion? What attributes of successful teachers do you think are teachable? Are there others that cannot be taught?

2. Do you agree with the following observation? If so, why? If not, why not?

   What a teacher does is more important for successful instruction than what she is. What can have a positive effect on instruction, therefore, are descriptions not of personal characteristics but of desirable actions.

3. The importance of teachers' constantly asking themselves, "*Why* am I doing what I'm doing?" permeated parts of Chapter 2. What examples of faulty instruction were used to illustrate the importance?

4. The significance for successful instruction of paying attention to small but important details was also highlighted. Recall from the chapter examples of failure to keep the significance in mind.

5. Over time, the classroom behavior of most teachers matures; for a few, however, it merely ages. Without question, those whose teaching ability does

improve with experience are the ones who work consciously toward improvement. What Chapter 2 says about instructional goals offers conscientious teachers some guidelines. See whether you can list them. (One possible list is at the end of the Review.)

6. Let me return to discipline problems since they are always high on the list of teachers' major concerns. Following Chapter 1, you were asked to list four procedures that were shown in the chapter to be causes of behavior problems. Your list should look something like the following:

   (a) Scheduling rest periods
   (b) Naming the undesirable behavior of a child (which encourages similar behavior in others)
   (c) Overstimulating children
   (d) Having one child write at the board while others wait

Chapter 2 pointed up still more ways in which teachers may unintentionally foster discipline problems. Add them to your list. Once the list is complete, you'll want to keep it in mind when you're teaching.

ANSWERS

(a) An instructional goal should be selected only if it matches what an individual or a group needs and is ready to learn.

(b) Once selected, a goal must be kept in mind, for it should affect not only what is done to accomplish it but also how it is done.

(c) Some goals can be attained through unexpected happenings; with others, carefully planned instruction is necessary.

CHAPTER

3

Readiness for Beginning Reading

PREVIEW

Individualized instruction has been defined as any instruction that deals with what an individual or a group needs and *is ready* to learn. "To be ready" is to have whatever it takes (understandings, abilities, experiences, motivation, etc.) to learn or to accomplish something.

Although readiness has as much significance for a college instructor as it does for those who work with four- and five-year-olds, Chapter 3 only attends to one of its aspects. It deals with the question, When are children ready to begin to learn to read? As it does this, the chapter will show the complexity of the question, thus the foolishness of simple answers.

To reveal the complexity, many different subtopics are discussed. Minimally, reading the chapter should allow you to:

1. Define readiness for beginning reading
2. See implications of the definition for instructional programs
3. See how a child's readiness can be assessed

It is possible, of course, that your own conception of readiness for beginning reading and of how it can be assessed is different from the one that underlies Chapter 3. If that is so, persistent comparisons of your ideas with those in the chapter will add to your comprehension. The same comparisons should also add depth to your understanding of your own point of view. Thus, nothing will be lost and much may be gained by a careful reading of Chapter 3.

When are children ready to begin to learn to read? is a question that has been debated for decades. That is why this chapter starts by looking at the reading readiness concept from a historical point of view.

THE TRADITIONAL VIEW OF READINESS

The term *reading readiness* first appeared in the professional literature in the 1920s. To explain how it was initially defined and why it was assigned this definition, developments that occurred even earlier need to be mentioned. At first they will seem far removed from the question of when children are ready for reading. Soon, though, you will see how all the pieces fit together and, in particular, how they account for the original interpretation of readiness.

Emergence of the Reading Readiness Concept

In American schools, a close association has always existed between starting school and starting to read. Because the age of six has been the common criterion for admission into first grade, a parallel development has been the expectation that "being six" and "starting to read" will occur simultaneously.

A study of some very early reports and articles concerned with reading identifies well-known scholars who objected to the idea that entrance into school should automatically mean the start of reading. Edmund Huey, best known for his 1908 text *The Psychology and Pedagogy of Reading* (41), quotes John Dewey as recommending the age of eight as an appropriate time to begin reading. But he also emphasizes that Dewey was objecting as much to the mechanical and passive way in which the schools taught this skill as he was to the time when they initiated instruction.

Huey's own objections were also directed as much to the nature of existing instruction as to the time when it began. He especially complained about the "unnatural" ways in which the schools introduced children to reading. He added specificity to his complaint by describing as a contrast the "natural, every-day activities" of the preschool child that sometimes teach him to read. As can be seen in the following quotation, Huey's language is a little old fashioned, but the theme in his 1908 description of preschoolers is strictly up to date:

> The child makes endless questionings about the names of things, as every mother knows. He is concerned also about the printed notices, signs, titles, visiting cards, etc., that come in his way, and should be told what these "say" when he makes

inquiry. It is surprising how large a stock of printed or written words a child will gradually come to recognize in this way. [41, p. 313]

While it is true that a few educators spoke out against the routine practice of initiating school instruction in reading at the start of first grade, it still must be concluded from a study of the literature that the years from 1900 to 1920 were relatively quiet about when to begin. Soon afterward, however, books and journals became heavy with questions and answers about the best time to start teaching reading. Why the change?

One of the most important, though indirect causes was the testing movement of the 1920s and 1930s. During that period, educators became interested in the scientific measurement of a child's behavior and achievements, and an unusually large number of tests were developed (65). Among the results of what became almost a craze to measure everything was the appearance of school surveys. Of relevance here is a finding that was common to many of them: large numbers of children were failing first grade, most often because of insufficient achievement in reading (16, 40, 57).

Within a short time, concern about this finding was widespread for at least two reasons. Successful teaching of reading, then as now, was considered uniquely important among elementary school responsibilities. In addition, the failures resulted in first-grade classrooms populated by a number of "over age" children. Behavior problems blossomed; so did concern about why first graders were having difficulty learning to read.

Logically, a study of reading problems—at any grade level and in any period of time—would look to such multiple, commonsense causes as inadequate teacher preparation, poor instruction, inappropriate instructional materials, large classes, low IQs among the children, and, perhaps, a lack of motivation. In the study of beginning reading problems that went on in the 1920s and 1930s, however, the factor given *singular* attention can be found in a pronouncement that appeared frequently in the professional literature of that period: First graders are having difficulty learning to read because they were not ready when instruction began. Why beginning reading problems were attributed so exclusively to a lack of readiness and why delaying instruction was soon proposed as the remedy can be understood only when the broader psychological and educational setting of the 1920s and 1930s is brought into focus. The following sections will sketch this period, highlighting developments that had a distinct effect on the way beginning reading problems were "explained."

Psychological Beliefs that Fostered the Traditional Interpretation of Readiness

To show why readiness received uncommon attention in the 1920s and 1930s, it is necessary to go back to still earlier decades in order to bring the name G. Stanley Hall into the discussion. Hall was a psychologist who, because of his reputation and numerous publications, had a striking influence on psychological interpretations of human behavior during the beginning years of this century. Prominent in Hall's writings was his belief in the unique importance of heredity in the development of a human being. Equally prominent was his acceptance of the theory of recapitulation (55). To point up the tenets of the theory, the following quotation from one of Hall's own texts is useful:

> The most general formulation of all the facts of development that we yet possess is contained in the law of recapitulation. This law declares that the individual, in his development, passes through stages similar to those through which the race has passed, and in the same order. [33, p. 8]

Hall's emphases on the unique importance of heredity and on recapitulation theory led to a view of man that stressed a *predetermined nature that unfolds in stages.* This interpretation of growth and development had a pronounced effect on the thinking of Hall's students, who included prominent individuals such as Frederick Kuhlmann, Lewis Terman, Patty Smith Hill, and Arnold Gesell. Because Gesell's work is so directly related to the concept of readiness, and because his writings were so influential during the 1920s and 1930s, he must get special attention in this attempt to explain why (a) lack of readiness and (b) postponed instruction were once viewed as the cause and the solution for beginning reading problems.

Arnold Gesell was a physician, thus his special interest in the maturation process is no surprise. Nor is his description of maturation in terms of distinct stages, since it clearly shows the influence of G. Stanley Hall (28, 29, 30, 31). Hall's influence seems even greater in Gesell's proposed explanation of the maturation process. Here, as Gesell and his students tried to account for developmental stages in children, they detoured away from factors like practice and learning and, instead, gave the credit to what they called at various times "intrinsic growth," "neural ripening," and "automatic and unfolding behavior."

Having read the foregoing sketch of the psychological climate of the 1920s, you should now understand why the first-grade reading problems uncovered in the surveys referred to earlier were "explained" with a reference to a lack of readiness rather than to such possible causes as poor instruction, excessively large classes, or inappropriate materials. The reasoning behind such an explanation can be outlined as follows:

EARLY INTERPRETATION OF BEGINNING READING PROBLEMS

1. Development takes place in stages that follow one another in an inevitable order.

2. Growth from one stage to another results from maturation (internal neural ripening), which occurs automatically with the passing of time.

3. The ability required to learn to read occurs at one of these stages.

4. Reading problems disclosed by the surveys suggest that most beginning first graders have not yet reached that stage of development and, therefore, are not yet ready to learn to read.

5. The solution is to postpone reading instruction so that with the passing of time, the children will mature and thus reach the stage of development that allows for success with reading.

As the next section will show, the traditional interpretation also asserts that the stage of development that allows for success with beginning reading is defined by a mental age of approximately 6.5 years.

Mental-Age Concept of Readiness

Given the circumstances of the 1920s, it would have been unusual to be content with a concept of readiness that related it to a vaguely defined stage in a child's development. After all, that hardly reflected the interest in exact measurement that characterized the Testing Movement. Not surprising, therefore, are the efforts that were soon made to define with more precision that stage of development thought to ensure a child's readiness for reading.

The form these efforts took was influenced by the appearance of group intelligence tests, because with their availability came many reports about the relationship between a child's intelligence and his reading achievement. Commonly, the focus was first-grade achievement. As early as 1920, in fact, one writer was saying that the children who were having difficulty with reading and failing first grade were those with mental ages of less than six years (17). Subsequently, other authors in the 1920s moved toward proposals that would establish a certain mental-age level as a requirement for starting instruction (2, 40, 69). Arthur, for example, writing in 1925, said that a mental age of 6.0–6.5 years was "necessary for standard first-grade achievement" (2).

The kind of thinking about readiness that is reflected in these reports seems to have been crystalized in an article that was published in 1931 and that became widely known and uncommonly influential for a long period of time (50). Written by Mabel Morphett and Carleton Washburne, the report described the reading achievement of first-grade children when one particular method was used in one particular school system (Winnetka, Ill.). Based on the children's achievement as it related to mental age, the authors concluded:

It seems safe to state that, by postponing the teaching of reading until children reach a mental age level of six and a half years, teachers can greatly decrease the chances of failure and discouragement and can correspondingly increase their efficiency. [50, p. 503]

How seriously Washburne took his own proposal is reflected in an article he wrote in 1936 called—quite in keeping with the prevailing psychological views —"Ripeness." He observed:

> Nowadays each first grade teacher in Winnetka has a chart showing when each of her children will be mentally six-and-a-half, and is careful to avoid any effort to get a child to read before he has reached this stage of mental growth. [66, p. 127]

Evidence of how seriously other educators took the Morphett-Washburne proposal is in reading methodology textbooks that appeared not long after their report, and also in those published as many as ten and twenty years later (9, 14, 18, 37, 39, 47, 49). In fact, some textbooks with publication dates of the 1960s were still taking it seriously (35, 51, 62).

Reasons for Acceptance of the Mental-Age Concept

Knowing how influential and long-lasting the mental-age concept of readiness has been, you might be wondering why findings from a study of one teaching method in one school system were accepted as being applicable to all children in all schools. Too, you might wonder why the acceptance persisted for so long. A subsequent section in the chapter will help with the latter question. Here let me deal with the one that asks why the Morphett-Washburne proposal was so readily accepted.

For one thing, their proposal fit in perfectly with the temper of the times in which it was made. It gave support to the "doctrine of postponement," because most children entering first grade do not have a mental age of 6.5 years. It also supported the notion that development proceeds in stages, and it honored the measurement and testing movement by being precise and "objective."

Any attempt to explain the unique influence of the mental-age concept of readiness must also take into account the prominence of Carleton Washburne. He was not only superintendent of the Winnetka schools—widely admired and copied in the 1930s—but also one of the most prestigious leaders of the Progressive Education Movement. As a result, what Washburne said was listened to— and not only in reading. Even earlier than 1931, he had made very specific proposals about what was to be taught in arithmetic and at which mental-age level (67). With all these facts in mind, neither his mental-age description of readiness nor the influence it wielded should come as any great surprise.

Early Objections to the Mental-Age Concept

Although the mental-age concept of readiness was widely accepted, a few objections were still raised. The most important came from Arthur Gates. Conclusions reached in two of his studies merit attention not only because they raised questions about the concept but also because they were in reports that appeared soon after the Morphett-Washburne article.

In May of 1936, in a report called "Reading Readiness: A Study of Factors Determining Success and Failure in Beginning Reading," Gates and Guy L. Bond described the reading achievement found in four first grades (26). Of relevance here is that in March they identified the ten lowest achievers and assigned them tutors. By June, all ten were enjoying success. Referring to that success, the authors wrote:

> The study emphasizes the importance of recognizing and adjusting to individual limitations and needs . . . rather than merely changing the time of beginning. It appears that readiness for reading is something to develop rather than merely to wait for. [26, p. 684]

In the same report they also pointed out:

> Correlations of mental age with reading achievement at the end of the year were about 0.25. When one studies the range of mental ages from the lowest to the highest in relation to reading achievement, there appears no suggestion of a crucial or critical point above which very few fail and below which a relatively large proportion fail. [26, p. 680]

The report concluded:

> The optimum time of beginning reading is not entirely dependent upon the nature of the child himself, but it is in a large measure determined by the nature of the reading program. [26, p. 684]

Another study reported by Gates in 1937 reached the same conclusion. This one had examined different methods of teaching reading and the achievement that resulted. Commenting on the findings, Gates observed:

> Reading is begun by very different materials, methods, and general procedures, some of which a pupil can master at the mental-age of five with reasonable ease, others of which would give him difficulty at the mental-age of seven. [25, p. 508]

As can be seen in these two research reports, a concept of reading readiness had emerged that was very much at odds with the Morphett-Washburne description. Within the Gates frame of reference, the burden of responsibility was moved to the instruction and away from the child. Questions were also raised about the wisdom of postponement and of equating readiness with a particular mental-age.

Essentially, then, Gates's message was: Improve your instruction and watch the children read! Apparently, the Morphett-Washburne proposal (Wait!) was more appealing. I say this because just as the publications of the 1930s and subsequent decades provide more than ample evidence of the prolonged acceptance of the mental-age concept of readiness, so too do they reveal how little attention went to Gates's findings. His simply did not move with the stream of popular thought.

SOME REVIEW QUESTIONS CONCERNING THE TRADITIONAL INTERPRETATION OF READINESS

Because a lot of ideas have now been covered in relatively few pages, this might be a good time to stop in order to see what has been comprehended. The following questions allow for self-evaluation.

1. In your own words, describe the traditional interpretation of readiness.
2. Using the time line shown below, explain the relevance of each of the following to the development of the traditional view:

G. Stanley Hall	Arnold Gesell	Testing Movement	Carleton Washburne
1900	1910	1920	1930	1940

3. Why can it be said that the discussion of readiness succeeds in showing that whether or not an idea is accepted depends as much on when it is proposed as on the quality of the idea itself?

VESTIGES OF TRADITIONAL VIEW OF READINESS

Knowing about the traditional view of readiness will allow you to see vestiges of the earlier interpretation in some current practices.

Motor Development and Readiness

Concern about the role played by physical maturation in readiness for reading continues to be apparent in what are usually called Readiness Checklists. A fairly recent one (59) includes the following item under the heading Motor Coordination:

1. Is the child able to perform the following tasks:
   a. hops on one foot?
   b. jumps?
   c. gallops?
   d. skips?
   e. kicks a ball?

The existence of highly proficient readers, young and old, who never could jump, gallop, skip, or kick a ball is enough to raise questions about the value of items like those listed above for decisions concerned with reading.

Other vestiges of the maturation emphasis are in currently available materials that provide training in skills described at various times as visual-motor, perceptual-motor, and sensorimotor. Names like Frostig (24), Getman (32), and Kephart (46) usually are associated with these workbooks, worksheets, and tests that have children perform such tasks as matching geometrical forms; tracing over lines arranged simply or in an assortment of mazes; identifying figures embedded in more complex figures; and adding to certain shapes and forms to make them look like others.

What motivates educators to choose these packaged programs is not research data, because they have never given any support to the contention that exercises like those mentioned above help children succeed with beginning reading (34, 36, 54). What does get support is that learning is specific, which means that learning experiences should be closely tied to goals. (For example, use letters, not geometrical shapes, to teach letter discrimination. Use words, not pictures, to help with word discrimination.) Applied to readiness, the same research adds credence to an assumption that underlies this and the next chapter: Readiness instruction is reading instruction in its earliest stages.

Reading Readiness Tests

A more visible and common vestige of traditional notions about readiness is the reading readiness test. Since these tests continue to be used by a large number of schools, they need to be discussed in some detail.

References to reading readiness tests appear in the literature as early as 1927 and 1928 (7, 63). Initial expectations for them are effectively portrayed in a 1927 issue of *Childhood Education*. Now, of course, the expectations seem naive.

> In the field of reading it is essential that a joyous attitude of success shall be cultivated from the first. This necessitates a stage of development in which the learner is capable of getting meaning from the crooked marks which symbolize ideas. When does this period come? . . . In which direction shall we look to discover the truth regarding this confused situation? Fortunately the scientific method points the way toward the solution of this and of other baffling problems. The first steps have been taken. First, the problem has been recognized. Second, a name has been coined for the characteristic which is sought, Reading Readiness, a term not only alliterative but meaningful. Third, tests are in process of developing which shall be applicable to any young child. . . . So we may look forward to the day when the measure of readiness will rest in objective tests and parent and teacher will both be governed thereby. [43, p. 209]

What did the tests that were "in the process of developing" turn out to be? They were group pencil-and-paper tests made up of various combinations of subtests. All such combinations typically included items dealing with vocabulary development and visual and auditory discrimination.

If a subtest focused on vocabulary, the children were usually asked to circle or underline a picture that went with a word named by the one administering the test, generally a teacher. Or the administrator might be directed by the test manual to read aloud a particular sentence; again, the children would be directed to select from a row of pictures the one that reflected its content.

Subtests for visual discrimination also relied on pictures. In this case, the *un*verified assumption was that if children noticed similarities and differences in pictures, they had the ability to see similarities and differences in letters and words. That the same questionable assumption held for geometrical figures also seems to have been accepted, because many of the early subtests focused on circles, squares, triangles, and so on. With these, a child would be asked to look at the first figure in a row and then to underline all the others that were the same as (or different from) the target shape.

Evidently, those who constructed readiness tests figured that sooner or later children would be taught phonics. This is suggested by the frequent inclusion of subtests dealing with some type of auditory discrimination. The kind most commonly tested focused on rhyme. In this case, the administrator might be directed to name each picture in a given row and to have the children underline or circle all the pictures whose names rhymed with the name of the first one. Sometimes, but less often, an auditory subtest dealt with the initial sounds of words. When this occurred, the one administering the test might say: "Put your finger under the picture of the door. I am going to name the other pictures in this row. Listen, because I want you to draw a line around the one whose name begins with the sound you hear at the beginning of *door*."

In addition to explaining how tests were to be administered, manuals also offered suggestions about the way results might be used. Almost without exception, one suggestion was to use them diagnostically. That is, school administrators and teachers were urged to study subtest scores in order to identify each child's strengths and weaknesses. Low scores showed what needed to be taught; high scores would indicate ways in which the child was ready for reading. What happened in practice, though, was something quite different. In practice, schools tended to use total scores to make global judgments. The end result was groups of first graders generally labeled "ready" or "unready."

What then? What came next depended on when the readiness test was administered; and dealing with that requires attention to reading readiness programs.

Reading Readiness Programs

When it was agreed in the 1930s that most children entering first grade were unready to read and that postponing instruction would ensure their being ready later, a decision had to be made about what was to be done while the children were "growing into readiness." The term used to describe the product of the decision was *reading readiness program*.

Content of Readiness Programs.   Although called by the same name, what went on at the beginning of the first-grade year varied considerably from school to school. Some of the variation, no doubt, reflected variation among teachers. But some also reflected differences in viewpoints about the very nature of readiness. Thus, educators who held staunchly to the notion that the passing of time *automatically* results in readiness also held to the idea that the content of a readiness program did not have to show a direct relationship to the reading process. On the other hand, those who believed that learning and practice made their own contributions to readiness had quite different conceptions of what the readiness program should be. Under their direction, its content was more likely to focus on goals similar to those assessed in readiness tests.

What also promoted attention to readiness test items—and this turned out to be uniquely influential over several decades—was the reading readiness workbook. Often, the publisher of a readiness test was also the publisher of one or more workbooks. Whether or not this was so, however, the content of the tests and the content of the workbooks were very similar. In time, the content of the workbooks and the content of the readiness programs were remarkably similar, too.

Duration of Readiness Programs.   In theory, a readiness program was for "unready" children and was to last until they became "ready." In practice, things were not like that. Instead, the typical procedure was to administer a readiness test (sometimes a group intelligence test was given, too) close to the start of the first-grade year. Evidently, the purpose was *not* to learn whether some children might be ready for reading but, rather, to see how much time all were to spend in a readiness program. The assumption seemed to be that it was good for everybody—ready or not.

If a school had decided that the shortest amount of time to be spent on readiness was, let's say, two months, then the first graders with the highest readiness and IQ scores were in a readiness program for two months. The remaining children participated for a longer amount of time, often determined somewhat arbitrarily and without consideration of particular children.

Other schools were more flexible about the duration of readiness activities. For instance, they might administer readiness tests more than once in order to make more frequent decisions about whether the readiness program needed to be continued for individual children. In such schools, nonetheless, total scores were still the concern. Probably very few schools ever used subtest scores diagnostically, carefully matching what was taught with what individual children needed to learn.

Reasons for Questionable Practices.   In retrospect, it is easy to be critical of practices like those just described. However, one must keep in mind some of the reasons for them. While such reasons do not endow the flaws with quality, they at least make them comprehensible.

Certainly one reason for many of the questionable practices was the large number of children typically found in a first-grade classroom when the readiness concept was in the spotlight. Ideally, readiness programs should have been highly individualized and should have included only children who seemed unready. Being responsible for large numbers of children—sometimes as many as forty—teachers were hardly able to achieve the ideal.

Further, the whole idea of readiness and of readiness programs was new. In addition, the programs were viewed not humbly but as a means of solving all the reading problems. No wonder they were greeted with enthusiasm that appears to have contributed to the notion that readiness programs are good for everybody, ready or not.

Why the content of the programs was often sterile and routine also has a very human explanation. When first-grade teachers were suddenly called upon to do something other than teach reading at the start of the school year, many, if not most, must have felt insecure to say the least. After all, a good program—whether for readiness or something else—is not created overnight. It is no wonder, then, that readiness workbooks received a warm reception and just about took over when decisions were being made about what to do with the time allotted to the readiness program.

Reasons for Maintenance of Questionable Practices.   Whereas it is fairly easy to see how questionable routines developed when readiness programs were a novelty, it is difficult to understand why they continued for so long. Yet, a number of reasons can be identified.

One is the tendency of schools to be conservative (68). They often want to hang on to what they are doing and sometimes even actively resist change. While some of the resistance, therefore, was part of what might be called "the human way," some also was connected with existing instructional materials—specifically, with the readiness workbooks that appeared shortly after the readiness programs began. The workbooks came—sometimes two and three to a set—as part of basal reader series. Because the basals had been used by the vast majority of elementary school teachers for many years, the readiness workbooks were used, too, and not always because their content taught what children needed to learn (3, 13). As one first-grade teacher explained to me not too many years ago, "Our principal buys the readiness workbooks, so we use them."

One other reason why certain practices connected with readiness continued for so long relates to another tendency among school people: to place too much faith in test scores. This certainly has been true of readiness scores in spite of the fact that researchers have questioned their predictive value almost from the time the tests came into existence. Although critics did have some positive effect on the content of revised editions, they had little effect on use. Readiness tests continued to be published over the years—and still are—apparently because they continued to be purchased by a large number of schools.

Still another reason for the longevity of certain practices connected with readiness assessment and readiness programs moves the focus away from the schools and toward psychology, because psychological conceptions of human growth and development changed very little from the early 1920s until the late 1950s. Supported by Gesell, his students, and his disciples, the popular view during the 1940s and 1950s was like the popular view of the 1920s and 1930s: Readiness for various tasks—including reading—results from maturation; therefore, the passing of time is the solution for problems connected with a lack of it.

In the 1940s and 1950s, support for such contentions came from psychologists other than Gesell. Willard Olson was especially popular among educators of young children, and his ideas about child development, expressed in terms of "organismic age," agreed with Gesell's (52, 53). Robert Havighurst, also well known to educators, offered no reason to question traditional practices as he wrote about "developmental tasks" and even referred to the notion of a "teachable moment" (38).

And so, having little reason to do otherwise, schools stayed with the routine practice of administering readiness tests in first grade and of having all the children—ready or not—participate in readiness programs. But then came Sputnik and what might accurately be called a revolution in education.

A NEW ERA

Although educational changes hardly occur on one certain day, it is now customary to designate the start of major, mid-century changes by citing the date when Russia launched Sputnik I: October 4, 1957. Predictably, the launching of a satellite by a foreign power produced a variety of repercussions in the United States. One was a criticism of public school education, increasing the tempo of the already existing debate about the quality of instruction in American schools (8). Now the debate stressed the inferiority of our educational endeavors compared to those of the Soviet Union (6, 15).

Resulting from this furor was an atmosphere characterized by the cry, "Let's teach more in our schools, and let's teach it earlier!" Such an atmosphere, as time has demonstrated, fostered rapt attention to new proposals from psychologists. Relevant to this chapter's consideration of readiness are those that highlighted both the learning potential of young children and the unique importance of the early years for intellectual development.

New Emphases in Psychology

One of the first books to receive the friendly blessing of the post-Sputnik era was *The Process of Education,* by Jerome Bruner (11). This was an account of a ten-day meeting "to discuss how education in science might be improved in our primary and secondary schools" (11, p. vii). In this book, Bruner gave special attention to the importance of the "structure of a discipline" in teaching that discipline to others. More specifically emphasized was the claim that the "fundamental character" of a discipline enables one "to narrow the gap between 'advanced' knowledge and 'elementary' knowledge" (11, p. 26). A chapter called "Readiness for Learning" was introduced by a statement that was to be quoted with great frequency: "We begin with the hypothesis that any subject can be taught effectively in some intellectually honest form to any child at any stage of development" (11, p. 33).

Those who took the time to read all of Bruner's book found the statement to have a meaning that was hardly startling. It simply urged in a somewhat different way that the schools take another look at how they organized and presented instruction in fields like science and mathematics. Nonetheless, when the pronouncement was quoted out of context—and it often was—it fostered wishful thinking about the learning potential of young children.

That was the beginning. Later, in 1961, a book by another psychologist became unusually popular. This one, *Intelligence and Experience,* by J. McV. Hunt, was a review and reinterpretation of earlier research (42). Among the large number of studies reviewed were those that had examined the effects of training and practice on certain aspects of development. According to the original interpretation, readiness to learn—whether a motor skill or an intellectual skill—was the product of maturation, not of training or practice. According to the new interpretation proposed by Hunt, a great variety of practices and experiences affected the emergence of a skill. Especially highlighted in his hypothetical explanation was the critical importance of *early* experiences.*

Given the broader concept of what constitutes "practice" and the new emphasis on the importance of early stimulation, it was natural that the young child's environment became a popular topic for discussion. Predictably, it provided the theme for still another book from which it became fashionable to quote. This one, *Stability and Change in Human Characteristics,* appeared in 1964 and was written by Benjamin Bloom (10). Like Hunt's work, Bloom's was a detailed reexamination of earlier research—in this instance, of long-term studies concerned with the development of certain measurable characteristics. Concluding that the most rapid period for the development of many characteristics—including intelligence—is in the first five years of life, Bloom again stressed the crucial importance of a child's early environment.

New Social Concerns

At the start of the 1960s, in the midst of the excitement about the importance of early environmental factors, another development occurred. It was a new interest

---

* To understand and appreciate the new interpretation, one must read the whole of Hunt's book *Intelligence and Experience* (42).

in an old problem: children from the lowest socioeconomic levels start school with disadvantages that prohibit adequate achievement. This concern was unusually vocal and widespread in the 1960s because of the political, social, and economic climate of the times (61). The concern led to plans for prekindergarten schooling for "culturally disadvantaged" children (plans later formalized in Head Start programs), a solution that reflected the psychological climate. Also reflecting it was a 1966 statement by the Educational Policies Commission of the National Education Association (23):

> A growing body of research and experience demonstrates that by the age of six most children have already developed a considerable part of the intellectual ability they will possess as adults. Six is now generally accepted as the normal age of entrance to school. We believe that this practice is obsolete. All children should have the opportunity to go to school at public expense beginning at the age of four. [23, p. 1]

Changes in the Timing of Reading Instruction

Given this collection of new emphases, it was only natural that the post-Sputnik years heard many complaints about the traditional interpretation of reading readiness. After all, an era that supported "the earlier the better" was not likely to be patient with school practices that postponed reading instruction beyond the start of first grade on the assumption that the passing of time will automatically ensure readiness for it.

As the years have shown, the typical response stemming from the impatience was neither complicated nor imaginative. For the most part, schools simply altered the timing of traditional practices. Readiness tests were administered earlier, often in kindergarten, where readiness workbooks could be found, too. In first grade, reading instruction usually started sooner—although readiness programs still were in some first-grade classrooms, especially in school districts that had no kindergartens. In a few places, the difference in timing was more radical: reading was introduced in kindergarten.

Results of the Changes

What was learned from the changes? Not much. The greatest difference, reading in the kindergarten, was not usually accompanied by changes in materials or methodology. Instead, they tended to be like what existed in a typical first grade (1, 5, 44, 45, 60, 64). As a consequence, restrictions were placed on what could be learned both about earlier reading and about the basic nature of readiness. The result is that the 1960s, with all their excitement about young children and earlier learning, contributed little to what could have been an enlightened discussion. Therefore, the concept of readiness to be proposed now cannot claim to have its roots in research-based facts. Nevertheless, it still will get detailed attention because everything I know about children, reading, and instruction supports it.

PROPOSED DEFINITION OF READINESS

The concept of readiness I offer is not an original one. It was articulated by Gates in the 1930s and at least inferred by others since then. In 1959 it was stated very effectively by Ausubel in an article in *Teachers College Record* (4). Although the concern of the article was not reading, Ausubel's description of readiness for any learning is useful for the present discussion.

Readiness, Ausubel proposed, is "the adequacy of existing capacity in relation to the demands of a given learning task" (4, p. 246). Let's examine the details of this definition to see what they say about requirements for success with beginning reading.

Existing Capacity.   Nothing that we know about humans indicates that heredity alone accounts for an individual's capacity to learn, nor does anything or anyone insist that only environmental factors determine it. At various times, it is true, either nature or nurture has been placed on a special pedestal of honor. Even amidst the adulation, however, the one not getting attention was never cast aside completely. The assumption of this discussion, therefore, is that each child's capacity at any given time is the product of an interplay among genetic endowment, maturation, experiences, and learnings. Just how this interplay takes place awaits a definitive explanation. For now, it seems correct to say that a child's attained capacity at any given time is something he has inherited, grown into, and learned.

Demands of the Learning Task.   What learning to read demands, or requires, of children varies from situation to situation. One reason for the variation is the selected teaching method. A beginning approach that expects children to remember the identity of whole words—to cite one illustration—has ability requirements that are different from another approach that stresses letter-sound relationships.

But even when the method is the same, requirements for success may vary. This is so because the quality of the instruction also is critical—as we all know, since we've all had personal experiences with good and poor teaching. Applied to beginning reading, the point is that what teachers do with a method and how well they do it help determine what is necessary for successful learning.

In other words, what learning to read demands of children is dependent upon both the kind and the quality of the instruction that is offered. This means that what it takes to be ready to read depends upon the instructional program.

Adequacy of Capacity in Relation to Demands.   One of the most important features of Ausubel's definition—important because it is usually neglected—
is the explicit attention it gives to the relational aspect of readiness. It reminds
us, simply but effectively, that the question of a child's readiness for reading has
a twofold focus: (a) the child's abilities *in relation to* (b) the instruction that
will be available. Practically speaking, this relationship means that "Is the child
ready?" is an incorrect question because it is incomplete. Instead, the concern
ought to be, "Is the child ready for this particular instructional program?"

Implicit in all these observations is that we really need to think in terms of
readinesses for reading, since some abilities will be prerequisites for one program
whereas a somewhat different collection might be necessary for another one. The
twofold focus also points up the folly of thinking that readiness is a uniform list
of abilities that can be assessed in something like a readiness test.

HOW SHOULD READINESS BE ASSESSED?

Readiness testing continues to go on in many elementary schools. An alternative
method is assessment with learning opportunities. Let's now consider each kind.

Assessment with Readiness Tests

As was explained earlier in the chapter, readiness tests are composed of subtests
that typically deal with matters such as visual discrimination, auditory discrimination, and vocabulary. Thus, they yield subtest scores as well as total scores. A
subtest score is sometimes referred to as a *profile* score because it supposedly reveals something specific about a performance. Total scores, on the other hand,
are called *composite* scores, since they are a collection of smaller pieces—that
is, of subtest scores.

Traditionally, total scores from readiness tests have been used to decide
whether children are ready or unready for reading. I believe two major flaws
characterize this use. First, it fails to recognize that different kinds of instruction
require different abilities and understandings. Second, it ignores that how a given
kind of instruction is carried on also affects what is required for success.

Still another flaw in using composite readiness scores to decide who is, and
who is not, ready for reading is that the user makes a questionable assumption;
namely, that when reading instruction does get underway, children will have to
learn everything immediately. This, however, contrasts sharply with the reality of
classroom instruction, which proceeds one small step at a time (a little today, a
little more tomorrow). Instead of being concerned only about what will be required *at the very beginning,* those who rely on composite scores to assess readiness appear to be looking at considerably more.

What they do *not* look at, on the other hand, is the possibility that coping with a readiness test may be more difficult than coping with beginning reading instruction. As mentioned, this first came to my attention when I had the chance to compare readiness test scores achieved by beginning first graders who had begun to read with those attained by classmates who had not (20). At first, it was surprising to see that some nonreaders did better than some readers. After a little reflection, however, the surprise vanished. The nonreaders had been in a kindergarten that offered readiness activities, usually in the form of completing workbook pages. This made them very familiar with the format, the language, and the content of the readiness test. In contrast, the children who were able to do some reading had been in a kindergarten that bypassed conventional readiness activities and, instead, involved the children in a reading program that progressed in a slow, carefully planned way. The result was readers, but not children who always did exceptionally well on a readiness test.

Thus far, only total scores have been considered. What about using subtest scores?

Authors of readiness tests commonly describe subtest scores as a source of help in diagnosing particular strengths and weaknesses. Instruction can then build on the strengths and work on the weaknesses. What about this?

In theory, the proposal sounds fine; in practice, however, problems exist. To begin, test authors still do not agree about what constitutes essential subskills for beginning reading. This means that a serious diagnostic use of low subscores could lead to time being wasted on nonessentials. Similar use of high scores, on the other hand, could foster unwarranted expectations, because what a child was able to do may not be very important for success with reading.

Other kinds of disagreement become apparent when different readiness tests are compared (58). Similar subtests are sometimes called by different names, and identical names are sometimes assigned to tests dealing with different abilities. Both types of discrepancies could foster inappropriate instructional remedies unless those fashioning them took the time to go beyond subtest labels in order to see what was actually being assessed.

Calfee and Venezky have concluded that an even greater problem exists when a tested ability is lacking but the remedy is not apparent (12). They ask, What is the implication for instruction when children are unable to identify a short-haired dog from among poorly detailed pictures of a Doberman, a Saint Bernard, and a cocker spaniel? What is a teacher supposed to do when children fail to select a picture of a jet airplane when the given task is to find the vehicle that carries the most people? A more basic question is, What does all this have to do with beginning reading?

While all these problems should be enough to raise questions about the diagnostic value of subtest scores in readiness tests, statistical considerations raise still more. From that perspective, the limited number of items typically composing a subtest do not allow for reliability, which means that retesting could result in a different score for the same child. Further, intercorrelations between subtests are usually so high as to indicate that independent skills are not being measured.

To sum up, then, serious flaws exist in readiness tests whether total scores are used to decide who is ready to begin to read or whether subtest scores are used to plan the details of instructional programs.

Having laid out all the problems that are associated with readiness testing, let me now describe what I believe is a far superior way to learn about children's readiness for reading.

Assessment with Learning Opportunities

The alternative method of assessment stems directly from Ausubel's definition of readiness (see Figure 3–1).

If, as Ausubel suggests, readiness is the adequacy of existing capacity in relation to the demands of the learning task, it follows that the best way to test for adequacy is to give children opportunities to learn to read in order to see what their capacity actually is. These opportunities should vary in methodology, because a child may be able to succeed with some methods but not with others. By observing what individual children do or do not learn from each method, much can be gleaned about their readiness and the kind of instruction that makes best use of their abilities and interests.

You might now be wondering what this recommendation would look like were it carried out in a classroom—say, in a kindergarten. Let me show you with

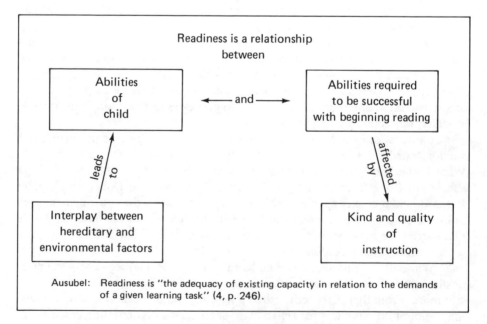

Figure 3–1. Ausubel's Definition of Readiness

illustrations featuring typical kindergarten activities. (The next chapter will show how these activities can be scheduled.)

Some time in every kindergarten goes to the job of taking attendance. Mundane though it is, attendance taking can be an opportunity for five-year-olds (or four-year-olds) to learn to read and for a teacher to learn something about existing capacities. Specifically, at the beginning of the year the teacher could take attendance by showing the children their first names on cards. Later in the year, the children could indicate their presence by selecting their name card and putting it on an attendance board. This simple routine could teach the children to read their names and probably others' names as well. In addition, it helps an observant teacher learn which children remember (read) names easily, which have some difficulty, and which remember few if any names.

Art activities are an example of another approach. In addition to being valuable forms of free expression, finished products in art can be a reason for kindergartners to learn to print their names and, later, to write captions and to read those composed by others. Pertinent to the theme of assessment is that these activities give a teacher the chance to identify children for whom writing and spelling might be an easy way into reading, to identify those who remember whole words with a minimum of exposure to them, and to become aware of children for whom the motor skill of writing is a formidable task or for whom it is difficult to compose even the briefest of captions.

Reading to children, still another kindergarten activity, should always be for enjoyment; but occasionally a story can be used as a vehicle for learning still more about the children's readiness for reading. Let's say, for example, that a couple of stories have been about Ping, a duck. Let's also say that two children in the class are named Paul and Penny. In such a case, a kindergarten teacher might one day decide to print *Ping* on the chalkboard and then ask, "Does anybody [pointing to *P*] have a name that starts the way *Ping* starts? If you do, I'll write your name up here with Ping's." Soon the board shows:

> Ping
>
> Paul
>
> Penny

Other questions (their number and kind will depend upon the children's abilities and interest) follow: "Does anybody know the name of the letter [pointing to *P*] at the beginning of these three names? . . . Have you ever seen any other word that begins with this letter *P*? . . . Now we have five words that begin with *P*. I'll read them all. As I do, listen to see if you can hear how they all start with the same sound. . . . Can someone tell us the sound that these names start with? . . . I'll say these words again. Watch how I put my lips together when I start to say each of them. Listen to the way each word starts. . . . Can someone tell us the sound that's at the beginning of all these words? . . . Can someone think of other words that start the way *Ping* and *Paul* and *Penny* and *Punch* and *Pat* begin? If you can, I'll write them up here, too."

On another day, another word and letter might be singled out for attention. Or the teacher might decide to repeat the attention given *P,* using a different collection of words to illustrate the sound it commonly stands for. Whatever the decision, the opportunity exists for children to respond and for a teacher to identify those who know letter names and even have skill in auditory discrimination. At the same time, the teacher also is likely to become aware of other kindergartners who appear to have no knowledge of letter names or, more likely, no understanding of what is meant by "begin with the same sound."

Perhaps these few illustrations of ordinary activities are enough to give specific meaning to what has been proposed as a way to assess children's readiness for reading: Give them varied opportunities to begin, and note what they are able to learn.

Implied in the illustrations are still other ideas that are important for teachers. Probably the best way to deal with them is through descriptions of two children who were present when the teacher in the kindergarten class just referred to wrote *Ping, Paul* and *Penny* and asked questions about them. We'll call the children Paul and Mary Anne.

Paul.   Paul has all the signs of being mentally slow. Even his physical movements are sluggish and awkward. When the teacher wrote *Ping* on the board and asked whether anyone had a name that began with the same letter, he remained silent. A concentrated look from the teacher plus a nudge from the child sitting next to him (Mary Anne) led to Paul's volunteering his name. It is doubtful that he ever would have mentioned it had there not been these hints from others. Once his name appeared on the board he seemed interested in the discussion, although he remained silent. The question now is, What meaning did the discussion and questioning have for both Paul and the teacher?

For his teacher, the situation gave further evidence of Paul's slowness. Even though the letter being highlighted was in his name, and even though he had seen it written many times before, he didn't seem to be aware that his name and Ping's began the same way. It was also unlikely that Paul had any understanding—at least his behavior showed none—of the concept *sound alike* when applied to parts of words.

For Paul himself, the situation was very interesting because everybody was talking about his name. He didn't remember anyone telling him before—they had, actually—that the first letter in his name was *P.* And he didn't know until the day of the *Ping* lesson that other words started with the same letter.

Now, what about Mary Anne? What did the same discussion and questioning mean for her? Something quite different, as the following account reveals.

Mary Anne.   Mary Anne is an alert child who doesn't believe in hiding her candle under a bushel basket. In the discussion of words beginning with *P,* she quickly informed the teacher that she knew its name because it was in her big sister's name (Pat). She said she could write her sister's name, and her mother's and daddy's names, too. As the discussion proceeded, she enjoyed making the sound of *P*—this seemed to be something new for her—and quickly recalled words beginning with it. *Punch, princess,* and *Pat* were her contributions when the teacher asked, "Can anyone think of some words that begin the way *Ping* begins?" (Mary Anne eagerly explained that *Punch* was the name of the detergent her mother used when she washed clothes.)

Obviously, what the discussion and questioning meant for Mary Anne was something totally different from what they had meant for Paul. With both children, though, the teacher had an opportunity to assess readiness. In the case of Mary Anne, much was learned—including that she had already begun to read, which is the very best behavioral sign of readiness. She also knew the name of *P,* enjoyed making the sound it represented in *Ping,* and was able to name words beginning with it. That she did some writing at home and was attentive to words in her environment also became clear.

While the teacher was looking for behavioral signs of readiness, what was Mary Anne getting out of the discussion and questions? Primarily, they helped her recall, and then use, what she already knew. New learnings seemed to be the understanding that words have a beginning sound and, secondly, that the sound that *p* represents is /p/. The teacher's assessment, then, turned into an opportunity for Mary Anne to have reading instruction; specifically, instruction in phonics.

What the same discussion and questioning turned out to be for both children is summarized in Table 3–1.

Table 3–1. Results of Ping Lesson for Two Children

	Assessment	Readiness Instruction	Reading Instruction
PAUL	X	X	
MARY ANNE	X		X

The table above and the descriptions of the two kindergartners offer the following important reminders for anyone who is concerned about assessing young children's readiness for reading.

ASSESSING READINESS FOR READING

1. A useful way to assess readiness is to provide children with varied opportunities to begin to read. What is or is not learned offers information not only about readiness but also about ways to teach reading that seem to be easiest and of greatest interest.

2. Assessment carried out this way provides more than just diagnostic information. It can result in readiness instruction and in reading instruction itself.

3. What any learning opportunity results in depends upon children's abilities. For some, an opportunity will only be preparation for reading. For other, more able children, it will be reading instruction.

One more point about readiness needs to be made. Let me make it by describing another child in the kindergarten that was just discussed.

Joey.   Joey is an enthusiastic participant in all activities. At the start of the year he generally went to the blocks at free-choice time, but quiet table games and puzzles soon became attractive. He also is an inevitable "joiner" whenever the teacher makes other choices available: "Today I'm going to be reading a story over in that part of the room" or "Today I'm going to be playing a game" (e.g., bingo played with numerals, letters, or words). When words enter into a game, Joey is involved and successful because of his ability to remember words with minimal help. He learned to read all the days of the week as a result of the quick, early-morning discussions related to "What day is today?" Because of the attention given to *September, October,* and *November* in connection with the calendar displayed in the room, he can read those words, too.

While using words in games, Joey's teacher has heard him make interesting comments. When *Sunday* was used he observed, "Sandy's name looks like a short Sunday." On another day, when the teacher wrote *silk* on the board while discussing fabrics and textures, Joey quickly observed, "That almost looks like *salt.*" Asked, "Where did you see *salt?*" he explained, "It's on our salt shaker at home."

To be especially noted for this discussion is that Joey's excellent visual memory is not matched by equal excellence in auditory discrimination. For instance, he rarely responds when the teacher makes requests like: "I'm going to say two words. Can you tell me whether they start with the same sound or a different sound: *ball, fence?* . . . I'm going to say some words. Can you tell me which of these words begin with the same sound: *mouse, table, mother?*"

What all these observations correctly indicate is that in certain ways Joey is more than ready for reading—he has already begun. In other ways, however, he is still learning to be ready. What the same observations mean more generally is that efforts to assess readiness should not have an either-or focus. That is, a teacher's thoughts ought *not* to be "Is he or is he not ready?" but rather "In what ways is he ready and in what ways is he not?"

This more correct concern has implications for the way we think about instruction. It reminds us—or should—that readiness instruction and reading instruction can go on simultaneously. With Joey, for instance, reading ability is developing as a result of help with whole-word identification. At the same time,

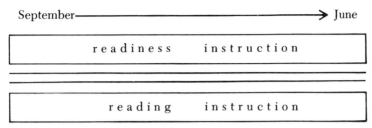

Figure 3–2. Simultaneous Readiness Instruction and Reading Instruction

the attention going to sounds is readiness instruction for him. Graphically, this point is shown in Figure 3–2. How different that conception is from the traditional all-or-none practice of separating the readiness program from the reading program (Figure 3–3).

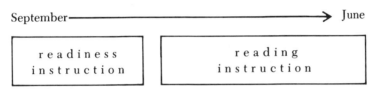

Figure 3–3. Readiness Program Separated from Reading Program

Still another important point is to be found in the observations made about Joey and the other children: readiness assessment is a daily occurrence, not a special event carried on at the beginning and end of each year. All the reasons why this is so have been summed up perfectly by MacGinitie: ". . . when a child is taught a little, he is then ready for a little more" (48, p. 399).

The disarming simplicity of MacGinitie's observation should not overshadow an important implication; namely, that beginners in reading are just that —*beginners*. As such, they do not have to be able to master *immediately* all that constitutes "reading ability." Instead, they achieve that ability piece by piece over a very long period of time. Practically speaking, this means that if reading instruction begins with the identification of a few carefully chosen words, the only requirement is the ability to distinguish among the words and, second, to remember what each says. If it happened—but this is unlikely—that each word began with the same letter and sound and, as a result, the teacher decided later to introduce a little phonics, then new requirements would come into existence: the ability to see that each word begins with the same letter and, second, the ability to hear that each begins with the same sound. With such abilities, a child is ready to be taught one letter–sound relationship.

Even these few comments should identify a major flaw in traditional questions and tests dealing with readiness. They appear to be concerned with the whole of reading ability rather than with the beginning steps that, when joined with many subsequent steps, *eventually* culminate in reading ability.

A BRIEF SUMMARY

The timing of beginning reading instruction has been the concern of this chapter. It merits detailed attention because a child's initial experience with any activity is of unique importance.

In considering the best time to start teaching reading, psychologists and educators whose views dominated the scene from the 1920s to the 1950s correctly gave attention to the concept of readiness. They asked, "When are children ready to be successful with reading?" Some answered, "When they have a mental age of about 6.5 years." Others turned to special testing as a way of finding an answer, and so was born the reading readiness test. Commonly, the interest of those who administered it was not in the possibility that some beginning first-graders might be ready for reading but, rather, in the question of how long each should spend in a readiness program, conceived of as being separate and distinct from the reading program.

The chapter went on to identify flaws in the early interpretation and use of the readiness concept. One was an exaggerated appreciation of the contributions made by heredity, maturation, and the passing of time. In contrast, the readiness concept proposed in this chapter assumes that readiness for reading is the product not only of genetic endowment and maturation but also of experiences and learnings. Within this framework, much about readiness is *teachable*.

Another point emphasized in the chapter is the need to look at instruction as well as children's abilities when readiness is being considered. With the two-fold focus, flaws can be seen in the question the earlier psychologists and educators asked—Is the child ready? It seemed to assume that success with every type of reading instruction demanded the same abilities and that readiness, therefore, could be assigned a single meaning.

This chapter tried to show that the correct question is more specific as it asks: Is the child ready to succeed *with this particular kind and quality of instruction?* Such questioning recognizes the equal significance of the child's abilities and of the instruction that will be available. Or, to put it somewhat differently, it reflects the relational aspect of readiness—an aspect effectively underscored in Ausubel's conception of readiness as being "the adequacy of existing capacity in relation to the demands of a given learning task" (4, p. 246).

This concept has implications for how readiness can be assessed: Give children varied opportunities to learn to read; what they do or do not learn tells something about their readiness as well as the way of teaching reading that takes advantage of their particular abilities and interests.

This type of assessment, the chapter showed, has the advantage of being two other things as well. It will be readiness instruction for some children and reading instruction for others. Because this way of assessing readiness makes use of different methodologies, teachers will also learn that *most children are neither totally ready nor totally unready for reading.* Such an awareness ought to encourage schools to give up the idea that "getting ready to read" and "beginning to read" occur at separate points on a time line, as well as the related practice of having a readiness program followed by a reading program. Instead, *readiness instruction* will be viewed as *reading instruction in its earliest stages.* One of the consequences of this could be a lessening of the gap that has traditionally existed between kindergarten and first grade.

As a result of some misguided efforts to close the gap, questionable developments have occurred in recent years. One is exemplified by kindergartens that have abandoned parts of their customary programs to allow time for the very practices that make some first-grade reading programs undesirable: large-group instruction coupled with an excessive use of workbooks, worksheets, dittoes, and drill. Visits to such classrooms tempt one to plead, "No reading, *please!*" The temptation is resisted only because other nursery schools and kindergartens demonstrate that preparation for reading, as well as reading instruction itself, can be carried on in ways that are both productive and enjoyable for the children. More about such programs later.

ONE FINAL COMMENT

In discussing readiness and beginning reading, this chapter has focused on school instruction. To be realistic, however, it cannot close without recognizing factors outside the school that also determine whether or not children succeed in learning to read.

For me, the key role played by nonschool factors was clearly underscored when I first attempted research. At the time, I was making a detailed case study of six first-grade boys who were in the process of learning to read (19). They had been selected because at the start of the year they were closely similar in chronological age, intelligence, socioeconomic background, and reading readiness test scores.

Although closely similar achievement in reading by the end of first grade seemed to be a reasonable prediction, the passing of time revealed something quite different. By June, the best reader among the six received a grade-level score of 2.9 on a standardized test—certainly encouraging for a first grader. In contrast, another boy scored at the 1.7 level; and still another only managed to get a score of 1.1.

Luckily, in addition to collecting various test scores and observing regularly in the classroom, I also conducted home interviews from which highly plausible explanations for the wide range of scores were identified. To illustrate, I learned that the highest achiever had a sister two years his senior who frequently played school at home. As often as she was a teacher, the mother of the two children explained, her brother was her pupil. Evidently she knew how to teach.

Other home-interview data revealed that the child who received the 1.1 score on the reading test was the only boy and the youngest child in his family, separated by twelve years from the next sibling. He had three older sisters, which, based on interview data, suggested he had been raised not by one mother but by four. The result was a boy whose most obvious characteristic was an incredible dependence. Since learning to read requires a certain amount of self-assertiveness, his lack of success would not be unexpected. Nor was the lower achievement of the boy who scored at the 1.7 grade level. During the first-grade year, his parents separated; by the end, they were in the process of getting a divorce. Several times during the home interview, this boy's mother mentioned how close he and his father had been and that the divorce was an especially traumatic experience for her son. Is it any wonder he was not overly successful with reading?

Admittedly, the children just described represent only an infinitesimally small proportion of all those who every year try to become readers. Still, they effectively demonstrate how life outside the classroom affects such efforts. Other nonschool factors—for instance, hyperactivity—also make their presence felt in classrooms and always prompt conscientious teachers to wonder, "What can *I* do to help?" Often, teachers and even parents can do little or nothing. For the former, the best chance to make a contribution lies in offering all children a superior instructional program. It is hoped that the rest of the chapters in this book will provide as much help as is needed to put together just such a program.

REVIEW

1. That skilled teachers are skilled observers was illustrated in Chapter 3. Especially highlighted was their ability to detect behavioral signs of readiness for reading. Such signs sometimes show up in unexpected places at unexpected times. To illustrate, while waiting in line in a grocery store recently, I watched a little girl approach a gumball machine. I judged her to be about three or four years old. Noticing the hand-printed sign that had been taped to the machine, she immediately asked a passerby, "What does that say?" Told that it said "out of order," she next inquired, "What does that mean?" Upon hearing the explanation, the child walked away, probably to look for her mother. What behavioral signs of readiness became apparent in that brief episode?

2. What Arthur Gates learned about readiness from his research and what David Ausubel implies in his definition of readiness are closely similar. Describe the similarities.

3. Let's assume that *you* are David Ausubel. How would you respond to the following letter written by a school superintendent?

> Dear Dr. Ausubel:
>
> We plan to teach reading in our kindergartens next fall and need to make decisions about which of our kindergarten children should participate. What readiness test do you think we should use to identify children who are likely to be successful?

4. Again, let's say that you're David Ausubel and that you have just given a talk to a group of educators. How would you respond to a first-grade teacher who made the following request during the question period?

> I teach first grade in a school where we're required to use the _____ basal readers.* All my children are doing well except for two boys who seem to be learning little or nothing. Evidently they're not yet ready for reading. What readiness materials would you recommend for them?

5. Even though readiness for beginning reading is not the concern of middle- and upper-grade teachers, they need to know something about it. For example, if a fifth-grade teacher was asked the following question during a parent-teacher conference, she ought to be prepared to respond. How would *you* respond to a parent who says:

> I have four children. My oldest is the brightest, yet she wasn't taught to read until some time after she started first grade. Now my youngest, who is five, is in kindergarten and she's learning to read even though she's not nearly as bright as her oldest sister. Why the difference?

6. When the readiness concept was being considered in earlier years, the notion of there being a "teachable moment" was often introduced into discussions. Do you think there is a particular moment when it is best for a child to begin to get help with reading?

REFERENCES

1. Appleton, Edith. "Beginning with Enthusiasm." *Education* LXXXVI (February, 1966), 347–349.
2. Arthur, Grace. "A Quantitative Study of the Results of Grouping First Grade Chil-

---

* The basal readers referred to start instruction by teaching phonics. The pace of instruction is fairly quick.

dren According to Mental Age." *Journal of Educational Research* XII (October, 1925), 173–185.

3. Austin, Mary C., and Morrison, Coleman. *The First R: The Harvard Report on Reading in the Elementary Schools.* New York: Macmillan Co., 1963.

4. Ausubel, David P. "Viewpoints from Related Disciplines: Human Growth and Development." *Teachers College Record* LX (February, 1959), 245–254.

5. Bacci, W. "Children Can Read in Kindergarten." *School Management* V (May, 1961), 120–122.

6. Benton, William. *This Is the Challenge.* New York: Associated College Presses, 1958.

7. Berry, Frances M. "The Baltimore Reading Readiness Test." *Childhood Education* III (January, 1927), 222–223.

8. Bestor, Arthur E. *Educational Wastelands, the Retreat from Learning in Our Public Schools.* Urbana: University of Illinois Press, 1953.

9. Betts, Emmett A. *The Prevention and Correction of Reading Difficulties.* Evanston, Ill.: Row Peterson and Co., 1936.

10. Bloom, Benjamin S. *Stability and Change in Human Characteristics.* New York: John Wiley and Sons, 1964.

11. Bruner, Jerome. *The Process of Education.* Cambridge, Mass.: Harvard University Press, 1960.

12. Calfee, R. C., and Venezky, R. L. "Component Skills in Beginning Reading." In *Psycholinguistics and the Teaching of Reading,* ed. K. S. Goodman and J. T. Fleming. Newark, Del.: International Reading Association, 1969.

13. Chall, Jeanne S. *Learning to Read: The Great Debate.* New York: McGraw-Hill Book Co., 1967.

14. Cole, Luella. *The Improvement of Reading: With Special Reference to Remedial Instruction.* New York: Farrar and Rinehart, 1938.

15. "Crisis in Education." *Life* XLIX (March 24, 1958), 26–35.

16. Dickson, Virgil E. *Mental Tests and the Classroom Teacher.* New York: World Book Co., 1923.

17. Dickson, Virgil E. "What First Grade Children Can Do in School as Related to What Is Shown by Mental Tests." *Journal of Educational Research* II (June, 1920), 475–480.

18. Dolch, Edward W. *Teaching Primary Reading.* Champaign, Ill.: Garrard Press, 1950.

19. Durkin, Dolores. "A Case-Study Approach toward an Identification of Factors Associated with Success and Failure in Learning to Read." *California Journal of Educational Research* XI (January, 1960), 26–33.

20. Durkin, Dolores. "A Six-Year Study of Children Who Learned to Read in School at the Age of Four." *Reading Research Quarterly* X, no. 1 (1974–1975), 9–61.

21. Durkin, Dolores. "When Should Children Begin to Read?" *Innovation and Change in Reading Instruction,* Chapter II. Sixty-seventh Yearbook of the National Society for the Study of Education, Part II. Chicago: Distributed by the University of Chicago Press, 1968.

22. Dykstra, Robert. "The Use of Reading Readiness Tests for Prediction and Diagnosis: A Critique." In *The Evaluation of Children's Reading Achievement,* ed. T. C. Barrett. Newark, Del.: International Reading Association, 1967.

23. Educational Policies Commission. *Universal Opportunity for Early Childhood Education.* Washington, D.C.: National Education Association, 1966.

24. Frostig, M., and Home, D. *The Frostig Program for the Development of Visual Perception*. Chicago: Follet Co., 1964.
25. Gates, Arthur I. "The Necessary Mental Age for Beginning Reading." *Elementary School Journal* XXXVII (March, 1937), 497–508.
26. Gates, Arthur I., and Bond, Guy L. "Reading Readiness: A Study of Factors Determining Success and Failure in Beginning Reading." *Teachers College Record* XXXVII (May, 1936), 679–685.
27. Gates, A. I.; Bond, G. L.; and Russell, D. H. *Methods of Determining Reading Readiness*. New York: Bureau of Publications, Teachers College, Columbia University, 1939.
28. Gesell, Arnold L. *The First Five Years of Life*. New York: Harper and Bros., 1940.
29. Gesell, Arnold L. *Infancy and Human Growth*. New York: Macmillan Co., 1928.
30. Gesell, Arnold L. *The Mental Growth of the Preschool Child*. New York: Macmillan Co., 1925.
31. Gesell, A., and Ilg, F. *The Child from Five to Ten*. New York: Harper and Bros., 1946.
32. Getman, G. N., and Kane, E. R. *The Physiology of Readiness*. Minneapolis: Pass, Inc., 1964.
33. Hall, G. Stanley. *The Psychology of Adolescence*. New York: D. Appleton and Co., 1904.
34. Hammill, D.; Goodman, L.; and Wiederholt, J. L. "Visual-Motor Processes: Can We Train Them?" *Reading Teacher* XXVII (February, 1974), 469–478.
35. Harris, Albert J. *Effective Teaching of Reading*. New York: David McKay Co., 1962.
36. Harris, Albert J. "Practical Applications of Reading Research." *Reading Teacher* XXIX (March, 1976), 559–565.
37. Harrison M. Lucille. *Reading Readiness*. Boston: Houghton Mifflin Co., 1936.
38. Havighurst, Robert. *Human Development and Education*. New York: Longmans, Green, and Co., 1953.
39. Hester, K. B. *Teaching Every Child to Read*. New York: Harper, 1955.
40. Holmes, Margaret C. "Investigation of Reading Readiness of First Grade Entrants." *Childhood Education* III (January, 1927), 215–221.
41. Huey, Edmund B. *The Psychology and Pedagogy of Reading*. New York: Macmillan Co., 1908.
42. Hunt, J. McVicker. *Intelligence and Experience*. New York: Ronald Press Co., 1961.
43. Jenkins, Frances. "Editorial." *Childhood Education* III (January, 1927), 209.
44. Keislar, E. R., and McNeil, J. D. "Oral and Non-Oral Methods of Teaching Reading." *Educational Leadership* XXV (May, 1968), 761–764.
45. Kelley, Marjorie L., and Chen, M. K. "An Experimental Study of Formal Reading Instruction at the Kindergarten Level." *Journal of Educational Research* LX (January, 1967), 224–229.
46. Kephart, N. C. *The Slow Learner in the Classroom*. Columbus, Ohio: Charles Merrill Co., 1960.
47. Lamoreaux, Lillian A., and Lee, Dorris M. *Learning to Read through Experience*. New York: Appleton-Century-Crofts, 1943.
48. MacGinitie, Walter H. "Evaluating Readiness for Learning to Read: A Critical Review and Evaluation of Research." *Reading Research Quarterly* IV (Spring, 1969), 396–410.

49. Monroe, Marion. *Children Who Cannot Read*. Chicago: University of Chicago Press, 1932.
50. Morphett, M. V., and Washburne, C. "When Should Children Begin to Read?" *Elementary School Journal* XXXI (March, 1931), 496–503.
51. Newton, J. Roy. *Reading in Your School*. New York: McGraw-Hill Book Co., 1960.
52. Olson, Willard. *Child Development*. Boston: D. C. Heath and Co., 1949.
53. Olson, W., and Hughes, B. "Concepts of Growth." *Childhood Education* XXI (October, 1944), 53–63.
54. Paradis, Edward E. "The Appropriateness of Visual Discrimination Exercises in Reading Readiness Materials." *Journal of Educational Research* LXVII (February, 1974), 276–278.
55. Partridge, G. E. *Genetic Philosophy of Education*. New York: Sturgis and Walton Co., 1912.
56. Pikulski, John. "Readiness for Reading: A Practical Approach." *Language Arts* LV (February, 1978), 192–197.
57. Reed, Mary M. *An Investigation of Practices in First Grade Admission and Promotion*. New York: Bureau of Publications, Teachers College, Columbia University, 1927.
58. Rude, R. T. "Readiness Tests: Implications for Early Childhood Education." *Reading Teacher* XXVI (March, 1973), 572–580.
59. Sanacare, Joseph. "A Checklist for the Evaluation of Reading Readiness." *Elementary English* L (September, 1973), 858–860.
60. Shapiro, Bernard, Jr., and Willford, R. E. "i.t.a.—Kindergarten or First Grade?" *Reading Teacher* XXII (January, 1969), 307–311.
61. Shaw, Frederick. "The Changing Curriculum." *Review of Educational Research* XXXVI (June, 1966), 343–352.
62. Smith, Henry P., and Dechant, Emerald V. *Psychology in Teaching Reading*. Englewood Cliffs, N.J.: Prentice-Hall, 1961.
63. Smith, Nila B. "Matching Ability as a Factor in First Grade Reading." *Journal of Educational Psychology* XIX (November, 1928), 560–571.
64. Sutton, Marjorie H. "Readiness for Reading at the Kindergarten Level." *Reading Teacher* XVII (January, 1964), 234–240.
65. Thorndike, R. L., and Hagen, E. *Measurement and Evaluation in Psychology and Education*. New York: John Wiley and Sons. 1969.
66. Washburne, Carleton. "Ripeness." *Progressive Education* XIII (February, 1936), 125–130.
67. Washburne, Carleton. "The Work of the Committee of Seven on Grade-Placement in Arithmetic." *Child Development and the Curriculum*, Chapter XVI. Thirty-eighth Yearbook of the National Society for the Study of Education, Part 1. Bloomington, Ill.: Public School Publishing Co., 1939.
68. Wayson, W. W. "A New Kind of Principal." *National Elementary Principal* L (February, 1971), 8–19.
69. Zornow, T. A., and Pachstein, L. A. "An Experiment in the Classification of First-Grade Children through Use of Mental Tests." *Elementary School Journal* XXIII (October, 1922), 136–146.

Early Instructional
Programs

As mentioned before, my initial contact with early readers was two longitudinal studies of children who learned to read before they started school (5).* At the time, attitudes toward early reading were anything but enthusiastic or supportive. Nonetheless, I was so impressed both with the children's abilities and with the easygoing, natural ways in which they had acquired them, that I developed a two-year school program based on what I had learned about the home reading (7, 8).

Although designed to teach reading, the school program had a language arts focus because (a) oral language (questions, etc.) had been encouraged in all the early readers' homes, and (b) some of the children had shown greater interest in learning to print than to read. In fact, it was through printing and asking questions about spellings that they started to read. The half-day program started with four-year-olds because the earlier studies revealed that age four is a common time for children to show an interest in print, both as something

to read and as something to copy.

The success of the program both in teaching reading and in promoting positive attitudes toward school fostered the conclusion that many—not all—pre–first graders are ready for reading and, second, that it can be taught in ways that are enjoyable and nonthreatening.

Between the time the program was initiated and the present, the field of early childhood education changed dramatically. While it has been wise enough to recognize the great learning potential of young children, it has been foolish enough to allow questionable developments to occur. Examples of the latter are now found in the large number of kindergartens (and even nursery schools) where teaching reading is equated with whole-class drill on phonics; and where the question, "But are they ready?" isn't even considered. Instead, materials are purchased, and the drill with everyone commences.

Chapters 4–6 are an attempt to counteract this packaged approach to teaching reading.

* References are at the end of Chapter 4.

CHAPTER

4

A Language Arts Approach for Beginning Reading

PREVIEW

Assigning the description "language arts approach" to what is recommended for beginning reading instruction is an attempt to emphasize that the foundation of reading is oral language. How a child's oral language enters into efforts to teach reading and efforts to learn to read is illustrated throughout the book.

Since the term *language arts* encompasses listening, speaking, reading, and writing, this is the time to define four terms:

Listening Vocabulary. All the words that a person understands when another speaks them constitute her or his listening vocabulary.

Speaking Vocabulary. All the words that a person can understand, pronounce, and use to communicate orally to another make up her or his speaking vocabulary.

Reading Vocabulary. A word is in a person's reading vocabulary if she or he can identify it in its written form and understand its meaning.

Writing Vocabulary. A word is in a person's writing vocabulary if that person is able to spell it, write it, and understand its meaning well enough to use it to communicate.

One way to show relationships among the four language arts is displayed in Table 4–1.

Table 4–1. Linguistic Communication

Productive Language Arts	Receptive Language Arts
Speaking	Listening
Writing	Reading

How attention can go to all the language arts in a beginning program is discussed and illustrated in the next three chapters. Before starting Chapter 4, you might want to read the summary at the end for an overview of its content.

The previous chapter showed how a variety of learning opportunities can allow for (a) assessment of readiness, (b) readiness instruction, and (c) beginning reading instruction. Also underscored was a fact that describes most pre–first grade groups: some members will have begun to read; others will need lots of help to get ready.

The bulk of the present chapter covers topics that will have greatest relevance for work designed to get children ready. Here, though, it is important to recall a definition offered earlier: readiness instruction is *reading instruction in its earliest stages*. What this chapter covers, then, are topics that concern the earliest stages of reading ability. To ensure maximum success at this beginning level, a language arts approach is recommended.

REASONS FOR LANGUAGE ARTS APPROACH

Since reading is the concern, some of you might wonder why the broader language arts approach *is* recommended. Won't it be inefficient? Doesn't it take time away from reading? Why not just teach children to read by concentrating on reading? Actually, the recommendation has to do with some facts.

The first fact is that the different aspects of language are interdependent. Instructors who rush to teach children to read even though they are barely able to speak or comprehend English, promptly learn about dependent relationships. And so do teachers who work with more fluent children. With the latter, for example, it is an everyday occurrence to see how much more readily they learn to read words that are in their speaking vocabulary than those whose meanings are vague or unknown. Awareness of the dependent relationships also flourishes when reading comprehension is the concern. Teachers quickly become aware that what cannot be understood when spoken cannot be understood when written. This is why it is accurate to say that the reading comprehension problems of some children are symptoms of more basic deficiencies in language.

Still another reason for recommending the language arts focus is that it encourages teachers of young children to give time to whatever aspect of language needs attention. In practice, this means that they are not likely to plunge children into reading (even though ability in reading might be a major instructional goal) when it is obvious that the children's ability in oral language suffers from serious limitations. I stress this point because I have visited classrooms in which teachers seemed to be guided by a very narrow view of what it means to teach reading or to prepare children for it.

To illustrate, I observed a kindergarten class in which the teacher was fortunate enough to have the sweet combination of a teacher aide and only eighteen children. Surrounded as this urban school was by extreme poverty and deprivation, my immediate thought as I entered the room was, "What a wonderful opportunity to help these children grow in their ability to use language!" Within a few minutes, my response was a combination of surprise and disappointment because in this classroom the aide assumed what I would call the role of a police officer. Both she and the teacher walked about the room, constantly reminding children not to talk—not even to ask questions—as they completed two pages in a reading readiness workbook. When I asked the teacher why the observed procedure was used, she responded without hesitation, "If these children are going to learn to read, they have to learn to be quiet." In this particular school, an explanation like "If these children are going to learn to read, they have to learn to talk" would have been easier to defend.

A more common disregard for the need to view reading in relation to other aspects of language is found now in nursery schools, kindergartens, and first grades. I refer to the unfortunate practice of drilling children on letters and sounds before they have had the chance to learn what reading and learning to read are all about. As their teachers follow manuals, use charts, and distribute workbooks and ditto sheets, basically important matters such as the connection between spoken and written language are bypassed, resulting in children who, in many instances, do not really know what the huffing and puffing and hissing are all about.

In addition to preserving the basic importance of oral language for reading, the language arts focus also allows for the likelihood that the easiest way into reading is different for different children. You will recall from Chapter 3 the description of Joey. With his wonderful memory, he easily recalled the identity of written words; yet he had difficulty with auditory discrimination. A language arts approach could accommodate him by providing multiple opportunities to learn to read words and also to prepare for phonics.

Another kindergartner (not mentioned in Chapter 3) could also be accommodated. His name is Frank. Unlike Joey, he shows little interest when the chance to learn to identify words is available, and he hardly gets excited when asked to think about words that begin with certain sounds. Frank, however, is very interested in learning to write and, in fact, has been printing at home since the age of four. Like other young "pencil-and-paper kids," his interest in writing is accompanied by a curiosity about spelling. Often, his question in school is, "How do you spell _____?" Although showing little interest as yet in reading per se, he is still doing some—thanks to the attention given printing and, when asked for, spelling. Eventually, Frank's teacher hopes to use his interest in printing letters to teach him about the sounds that some of them record. Meanwhile, his frequent decision at free-choice time is to print on one of the small chalkboards.

Paul must not be overlooked in this discussion of kindergartners. He is the child, you will recall, who is slow in everything. Yet he, too, can be accommodated in a program that puts reading into the context of the language arts. Such a context takes pressure off his teacher, for she feels no need to run to reading immediately and directly. It also helps her put Paul's needs into a correct perspective. He has a long way to go with oral language, thus needs a great deal of help and encouragement with that. Even while this is going on, attention is being given to such personally captivating words as his own name. Paul recognizes its written form, knows the name of *P,* and gets excited whenever he sees it in words displayed in the classroom. When instructional time goes to writing, his progress does not match his interest; nonetheless, he is able to make *P* and *l,* and the *a* and *u* are showing improvement.

Still another important kind of accommodation is facilitated when all the language arts are kept in mind. This one has to do with the very obvious fact that young children love nobody quite as much as they love themselves. Whether this reflects what Piaget calls the "egocentric stage" is less important for this discussion than whether teachers take advantage of the fact that young children love to listen to—and talk, read, and write about—themselves. Teachers who do not take advantage of these love affairs are foolish indeed.

The language arts perspective offers the wise teacher unending opportunities to use the factor of self-interest. Just consider the first names of children, for instance. I have watched one kindergarten teacher use a year-long interest in name cards (approximately 5 by 12 inches) not only for attendance-taking but also to give attention to instructional goals related to:

> spacing between words
>
> letter names
>
> capitalization
>
> printing
>
> letter sounds
>
> alphabetical order

In this classroom, one positive by-product of the children's involvement with names and attendance-taking was a heightened awareness of who was absent. As a result, an absentee's return to school was greeted with unusual enthusiasm, which surely must have contributed to that child's positive feelings about school.

One more advantage of a language arts approach should be mentioned. It is the possibility of its broader perspective becoming a means of steering away from the label "early reading program." This could be of monumental importance because such a label typically leads to the expectation that every child participating in the program *will* read. Whenever that happens, pressure is put not only on the children but also on their teachers. One common result is exactly what nobody should want for potential beginners in reading: routine and uniform instruction.

EXPECTATIONS FOR LANGUAGE ARTS APPROACH

All one has to do is visit nursery schools and kindergartens located in a variety of communities to learn that no single list of educational objectives will ever be appropriate for everyone in these age groups. I myself have observed in nursery schools in which some of the children were more linguistically sophisticated than others I had seen in first grades. And similar discrepancies are found in behavior. To cite one illustration, I used a day to observe in the kindergartens and first grades in one school. In the kindergartens, I saw children whose behavior suggested far greater maturity and independence than would ordinarily be expected of five-year-olds. Yet when I visited the six-year-old groups, I saw others whose behavior patterns were those associated with considerably younger children and would thus be a deterrent to their learning. All this is to suggest that the academic expectations established for any language arts program should vary from community to community, from school to school, and even from one group to another in the same school. In practice, such variation will result in programs in which no child is frustrated and, equally important, no child is bored. The variability in expectations means that all this book can do is suggest possible goals and some procedures for attaining them. In turn, readers must select whatever seems appropriate for the children they teach or will be teaching.

REQUIREMENTS OF LANGUAGE ARTS APPROACH

A language arts approach requires flexible scheduling, a pervasive language arts concern, and careful planning.

Flexible Scheduling

Just as it is unrealistic to think in terms of a uniform list of objectives for all instructional programs, so too is it unrealistic to think that one certain schedule is best for every situation. Still, teachers of young children do need to give time and thought to decisions concerned with who will do what and when.

Before one sample schedule is discussed, the importance of flexibility needs to be emphasized.

When young children are having their first experience with going to school, they must be given ample time to learn its routines as well as some of the do's and don't's of behavior. This means that only minimal attention can go to academic goals—although, as the illustrative material in Tables 4–2 and 4–3 will show (in section "Careful Planning"), even the start of a year allows for relaxed and personal attention to children's names, the names of colors, and so on. Nonetheless, much consideration needs to be given in the beginning to what might globally be called adjustment—in this instance, to new adults, to new children, and to new expectations.

In time (the exact amount of time will vary, sometimes considerably), increased attention can go to academic goals dealing with one or more aspects of the language arts. At first, it will take a long time for the children to do just a few things. Then, as time passes, more will be done more quickly. One consequence of such natural change and growth is the need for a change in the schedule, because a static one inevitably leads to idle and mischievous children.

The need for another kind of flexibility is reflected in the behavior of the teachers (at all grade levels) who persist in carrying out a certain instructional plan even when it is obvious that it is not going well. The children are not the least bit interested, or perhaps they are frustrated or bored. And yet the teacher continues.

Once, when I was working with a group of new teachers, one among them had this characteristic to such a degree that it caused discipline problems. When we talked about her tendency to persist come what may, she was very honest, saying she was aware of the problem but didn't have a solution. She explained that she panicked every time she had the feeling of losing the children but, not knowing what else to do, continued with her original plan. Since one plan plus three emergency plans for each instructional period was hardly a practical solution, I offered a much simpler alternative: keep books close by to serve as a security blanket. During a period set aside for letter identification, for instance, it would be appropriate to have an alphabet book available. Should it happen that what was planned for helping with letter identification did not work out or, perhaps, did not take as long as was anticipated, she could gracefully shift to the book to look at illustrations, name letters, talk about them, and so on.

Later, it was interesting to see how the available book added tremendously to this new teacher's security. In a very short time, as a matter of fact, the "blanket" was unnecessary. As she gained self-confidence and began to know the children better, her plans were almost always successful, probably because she put them together carefully and executed them with just the right amount of flexibility.

Sample Schedule.   The time when various things might be done in a half-day kindergarten program will now be discussed. Those of you who work in nursery schools or with first graders should find in this illustrative schedule bits and pieces that are appropriate and possible for your programs, too.

The schedule shown below was followed (with flexibility) in a kindergarten in which there were twenty-three children, a teacher, and an aide.

| 8:30– 8:45 A.M. | Conversation groups |
| 8:45– 9:00 | Attendance-taking; attention to date, weather, and current interests |

9:00– 9:20	Academic period for one group Free-choice for other group
9:20– 9:40	Groups reversed for above activities
9:40–10:00	Music
10:00–10:30	Playtime, bathroom, milk
10:30–11:00	Art
11:00–11:15	Storytime
11:15–11:20	Preparation for home

At conversation time, the children spontaneously divided into two groups of approximately equal size, although on some days the boys made up one group while the girls composed the second. The teacher sat around a table with one of the two groups, and the aide conversed informally with the other. (How conversation time can function in expanding listening-speaking vocabularies is discussed in Chapter 5.)

The next period of approximately 15 minutes began with attendance-taking and ended with current interests. All the children were together for this, sitting on the floor in front of the teacher. Meanwhile, the aide prepared materials for use later on in the morning.

At about nine o'clock, the academic goals of the program received explicit attention. (As will be shown later, more casual attention went to them at other times.) At the start of the year, the academic period on Monday was a time to provide help with color identification; soon afterward, it became a time to teach color words. Still later, Monday was the day when either extra help (with anything), or extra challenge was provided. On Tuesday, letter names and printing received special consideration, although attention went to both at other times, too. For the more advanced children, Tuesday soon allowed for help with simple phonics. (How letter-naming ability, printing ability, and beginning phonics can be taught is the subject of Chapter 6.)

On Wednesday, ready children were given carefully planned opportunities to learn to read some words, generally selected in relation to the children's interests or to current activities. As words were learned, sentences were constructed, and homemade books began to accumulate. Thursday was a time for the teacher to get her bearings and to do whatever needed to be done. The usual activity was work with small numbers of children who needed extra help or challenge, or who just needed someone to talk to. On Friday, the academic period singled out numeral identification for attention. This progressed with the help of materials like birthday cards, calendars, measuring tapes, license plates, television dials, clocks, store catalogues, and telephones. As the year moved along, simple mathematical concepts were introduced. Although not officially on the calendar, the teacher's special interest in word meanings pervaded everything in the daily schedule. In addition, she commonly used an academic period to do something special with meanings. (Teaching word meanings is one major concern of Chapter 5.)

While the teacher worked on the above activities with some children (selected on the basis of ability), the aide was responsible for the others. Her work was to supervise the activities selected by the children from among prescribed possibilities that included, at the very beginning of the year, blocks, trucks, dolls, dishes, telephones, and so on. Possibilities were gradually altered to include activities such as writing on small chalkboards or slates, working puzzles, and playing with sequence cards, concept cards, or bingo cards that, at different times, displayed colors, numerals, letters, and words. Eventually, three learning centers were established (Listening, Reading, Writing), and the aide divided her time among them. Then, children could be found involved with activities such as listening to stories on earphones, making signs for block constructions, dictating descriptions of their pictures to the aide, and playing with a variety of number and word games.

At approximately 9:20, the children who were with the teacher changed to free-choice activities; those who had been with the aide started their work with the teacher. (Ability groups varied, depending on instructional concerns.)

Music followed the academic periods and was a time for fun and relaxation. In ways that would not take away from either, songs were used occasionally to help with academic goals.

Next came playtime. For that, the children went outdoors whenever weather permitted. Bathroom and refreshment needs were taken care of afterwards.

For art, which lasted approximately thirty minutes, both the teacher and the aide worked with the children. Usually the teacher gave directions and then both she and her assistant distributed materials and, later, helped or talked with individuals. During art, the atmosphere was relaxed but never rowdy. Conversations among the children and between teacher and child were taken for granted. At times, art projects were also used to help with academic goals.

Next came a story, and then it was time to prepare for home.

While the assistance of the aide contributed substantially to the program just described, it could still function successfully without extra help. Certain things would have to be done differently, however.

For instance, at the start of the year, the children would have to be given time to learn to work independently. For a while, therefore, the teacher would supervise while the entire class was engaged in free-choice activities. Once the children seemed to know what was expected, the academic periods could begin. Whenever new free-choice possibilities were made available, more temporary supervision would be required, this time to make certain that everyone knew how the new choices were to be used.

Essentially, then, the program would be the same whether or not the teacher had an aide; but with an unassisted teacher, it would progress more slowly and probably less smoothly.

Pervasive Language Arts Concern

Since the discussion of the sample schedule made references to instructional periods, you might have concluded that language arts goals only get attention at stipulated times. Not so. The language arts focus that underlies this chapter pervades the whole of a program. It is a concern that should permeate teachers' thoughts, reminding them to be constantly searching for interesting and natural opportunities to give attention to any and all aspects of language.

Because of the special importance of this point, let me make it more graphic with illustrations that show that listening, speaking, reading, and writing need not be confined to specified periods. To begin, let me describe how art projects can sometimes be used to give attention to one or more of the language arts.

A kindergarten teacher, on the day she discussed the sound that *v* stands for with about half the class, had all the children make paper vases when art was scheduled. On each, she herself carefully printed the word *vase* and called the children's attention to the way it started with *v*. One child enthusiastically called everyone's attention to the fact that he knew about its sound, which he promptly identified. Since the vases seemed empty without flowers, the teacher suggested that on the following day paper flowers could be made to fill them.

When art began the next day, the vases were brought out. All the children were asked to look at *vase,* to spell it, and to make the sound of *v* if they could. Then the teacher commented that it would be a good idea to fill the vases with a flower whose name also started with *v*. Thanks to a grandmother who had a collection of some thirty violet plants, her grandson immediately suggested "violets." Not by accident, colored pictures of violets were in a drawer. They were taken out by the teacher and thumbtacked to a bulletin board. Beside the pictures went the word *violets,* and then the children began to make some for their vases.

In early April in another kindergarten, the teacher was especially pleased with the number of words most children had learned to read, but uncomfortable about the possibility of their forgetting everything they knew over the long spring vacation. To encourage the children to play with words at home, she decided to have them make Easter baskets which, during the course of the week before vacation, they would gradually fill with small, egg-shaped pieces of construction paper of various colors. On the day set aside for color identification, the children —in small groups—reviewed colors. As each child successfully named one, an egg of that color went into his basket. The same review and reward were used on subsequent days in connection with numeral identification, letter identification, and, for two days, word identification. The week thus ended with a review of material pertaining to four instructional goals—and, in addition, with well-filled Easter baskets.*

* I learned about this art project not from the teacher but from a parent of a girl in her class. Her mother told me that the Easter basket and eggs had become one of her daughter's most treasured possessions and that it was frequently used when she and her older sister played school together. Because playing school is a common occurrence with young children

Using more illustrations taken from classrooms, let me continue to demonstrate, now with the help of music, that instruction in the language arts need not be confined to prescribed periods.

In one nursery school class, the children began the year completely unfamiliar with the Alphabet Song. Consequently, it was taught early (and learned quickly). Sometimes the children sang it while they were having a midmorning snack; when they did, the teacher took the opportunity to discuss and hang up one more alphabet card. That was how all the cards eventually got on the wall. Later, either the teacher or a child pointed to the letters as the song was sung or listened to on a record.

One morning, as a special surprise, each child received an alphabet book. It was a three-page dittoed copy of the Alphabet Song arranged in the way shown in Figure 4–1. At first, the teacher and children talked about the page numbers 1 to 3 because they were known by almost everyone. Then the children were asked to point to the letters as the teacher sang part of the song very slowly. When they got to page 3, a few of the children quickly identified *I* and *me,* which were part of several earlier bulletin-board displays, so the teacher wrote those words on the board for all to see and say. Following that, she slowly sang the words on page 3, again encouraging the children to point to each letter and word as she sang. Before the books were finally taken home, covers were made by the children during an art period and often incorporated letters of the alphabet.

Later, when this same group arrived in kindergarten, most were able to name all the letters. Recognizing the omnipresent need for review, their kindergarten teacher soon found a rich opportunity to name many letters in connection with a popular song of the times—which, again, the children learned readily. You may remember the song if I just note the word that was written by the teacher and then spelled by fascinated children:

s u p e r c a l i f r a g i l i s t i c e x p i a l i d o c i o u s

In addition to helping with letter names, music can also call attention to words. In fact, because so many songs for young children have numerous verses, the combined use of words and pictures fits in naturally. Take "Old MacDonald" as an example. With all its verses, how natural to show a picture of an animal as a cue for the next verse to be sung. For the teacher who has the language arts in mind, the same pictures might later be labeled with the animals' names. And, as a final step, why not show the labels alone to indicate the next verse to be sung? All this, of course, would take place over several weeks, and would be interspersed with opportunities for the children to examine and discuss the pictures and to look carefully at the written names of the animals. Later, perhaps when the teacher decides to extend listening-speaking vocabularies by calling attention to pairs of words like *cow-calf* and *pig-piglet,* the pictures could be used again to

---

and older siblings, teachers should keep it in mind as they make plans for materials that will be taken home.

Name_____

    a   b   c   d   e   f   g

    h   i   j   k

    l   m   n   o   p

–1–

    q   r   s

    t   u   v

    w   x   y   z

–2–

Now I know my a b c's.

Tell me what you think of me.

–3–

Figure 4–1. Format of the Alphabet Book

promote discussion and questions and, perhaps, to add to a bulletin-board display entitled "Animal Words."

Probably these few illustrations are sufficient to show how the language arts can get attention at more than just the periods of time set aside for them. The illustrations should also have indicated that opportunities to learn language arts skills can be offered in ways that are personal, interesting, and free of pressure.

Careful Planning

If activities are to be academically productive as well as personal and interesting, they need to be carefully planned beforehand. This suggestion is not meant to minimize the importance or potential of unexpected opportunities. Rather, it is intended to emphasize that an effective instructional program will exist only when teachers put its pieces together with care and thought. What one nursery school teacher planned for color identification is in Table 4–2 (page 94). Table 4–3 (pages 95–96) shows a kindergarten teacher's plans for working early in the year on a variety of goals that capitalized on the children's interest in their own names. (Please take a look at the plans before proceeding with the chapter.)

SELECTING GOALS

If individualized instruction is to be achieved, goals must be based on what children do and do not know. At the start of a school year, learning what they know about the names of colors, letters, and numbers is helpful for establishing instructional groups. It can be accomplished easily and quickly with the help of an aide or an older elementary school student.

Assessing color-identification abilities begins with the selection of a given number of colors and progresses by asking children, individually and privately, "Can you tell me the name of this color?" Colors the children cannot identify are checked on a class-record sheet. In this way, what needs to be taught is clearly indicated.

On other days, diagnosis for letter and number identifications will progress in a similar fashion. Numbers from 1–10 (or, depending on the children, 1–20) are typed with a primer-size typewriter in random order on a sheet of paper. Children will be asked to name what they can. (For the sake of the children, the emphasis should be on what is known, not on what is unknown.) Again, responses should be recorded.

Letters are typed in random order in both lowercase and capital forms. The diagnosis might continue for several days (unless the children are quite advanced) so that an excessive number of letters is not covered at any one time.

Typically, some children will name every color, letter, and number, and

Table 4–2. A Nursery School Teacher's Account of Some of the Things She Did to Teach Color Identification

GOAL	PROCEDURES
To teach color identification	1. Named and discussed colors found in: a. name tags b. children's and teacher's clothing c. children's drawings d. bulletin board displays* e. traffic signs f. calendar pictures g. crayons, paints, clay, chalk h. construction paper i. cut-out train cars** j. autumn leaves k. soap bubbles made outdoors 2. Discussed colors during outdoor walks, giving attention to: a. houses b. flowers c. signs d. train cars e. rocks 3. Read books concerned with colors and discussed pictures.

* For first week of school, bulletin board showed large cut-out figures of a boy and a girl. Every day their clothing was changed (paper doll method), and color of new clothing was discussed.

** Made cut-out train of differently colored cars. Was first used to identify colors. Throughout the school year, each car became a month and children having a birthday during a particular month had their names placed on their car. The train was also used to show children the names of the months.

Table 4–3. A Kindergarten Teacher's Account of How She Used Children's Names to Attain Certain Goals

GOALS	PROCEDURES
1. To introduce school with a personal emphasis	1. Used name tags ("Hello" tags) for each child during first week. Used sheriff's badges for second week and bracelets during third week. 2. Took Polaroid picture of each child. Displayed on bulletin board with first names under pictures. (Later, taken home in envelopes marked with children's names.) 3. Used place cards on tables at milk time during early weeks.
2. To teach identification of first names	1. Printed first names on all papers. Encouraged children to print all or part of their names themselves. 2. Displayed name cards on two bulletin board displays: a. on balloons b. on large red house. 3. Gave smaller name cards to children to compare with cards on bulletin board. 4. Let children take own attendance by removing name cards from card holder. 5. Each day had children read names of those who were absent (or present).

Table 4–3. (Continued)

GOALS	PROCEDURES
3. To encourage attention to individual letters	1. Using large name cards, discussed names beginning with same letters. Named those letters. 2. Helped individual children look for words with letters that were in their names. Named the letters. 3. Gave each child white squares on which a letter in his name was written. Distributed name cards. Had children arrange letter-squares in a sequence to make their names. Had them paste letter-squares on paper. Later they drew a picture of themselves above their names.

others will know practically none. In between will be a large number of still other children whose abilities fall somewhere between the two extremes. Knowing all this about the children, a teacher is ready to start instruction based on needs and within the organizational schedule referred to earlier.

Meanwhile, other instructional goals will be kept in mind and attended to. The ones that are most important at the very beginning are listed below. Even though some young children will be beyond such goals—some far beyond—teachers need to be aware of what they are so that they will know where to start with beginners.

INSTRUCTIONAL GOALS AT THE VERY BEGINNING

1. Motivate children to want to learn to read

2. Help children acquire some understanding of what reading and learning to read are all about

3. Teach about the left-to-right, top-to-bottom orientation of written English

4. Teach the meaning of *word* and the function of space in establishing word boundaries

5. Teach children the meanings of terms that figure in reading instruction

6. Teach children to discriminate visually among letters and among words

7. Teach children the names of letters

To be noted immediately is that the list is not meant to suggest a mandatory sequence for instruction, nor should it be interpreted to signify that one goal must be fully realized before anything is done with another. Correctly interpreted, the list suggests what can be done concurrently, not sequentially. This means that on any given day, a teacher may be working on several of the listed goals.

What was *not* listed also merits a comment or two. Among the omissions is, "Give children opportunities to learn to read words." This was omitted because it is taken for granted that teachers are always looking for opportunities to teach words that are of special interest; meanwhile, for the less advanced children, they are giving conscious and careful attention to the listed goals.

Other goals were omitted because they do not contribute to success with beginning reading (1, 9, 11, 15). Here I refer to work in visual discrimination that concentrates on pictures and geometrical shapes; and to other fruitless activities that are supposed to prepare children for phonics—distinguishing among musical and environmental sounds, for instance. And, speaking of phonics, you may have wondered why teaching letter-sound relationships was not on the list. It was not mentioned because plunging into phonics at the very start presents children with some facts about language that are foreign and difficult for them to understand—for instance, that a word is composed of more than one sound; that a word has such things as a beginning sound; that words are recorded with letters that represent sounds. None of this is to say that pre–first grade programs ought to omit phonics instruction. To the contrary. Chapter 6, in fact, describes beginning phonics. It *is* to say, however, that teaching phonics is not the easiest or most interesting way to introduce children to the important job of becoming a reader.

To summarize, if the list of beginning goals steers teachers of young children toward important things and away from the irrelevant and the difficult, it will have accomplished its mission.

Since language experience materials provide one of the best means for realizing beginning goals, they will be discussed in detail later in the chapter. Now I want to deal with a topic that is often neglected; namely, the importance of knowing the language of instruction.

KNOWING THE LANGUAGE OF INSTRUCTION

Those who work with young children can both overestimate and underestimate what they know. Overestimating their understanding of words that enter into reading instruction is fairly common and leads to the use of terms that are either not understood or insufficiently understood. What results can be pinpointed with illustrations.

In one kindergarten, the teacher wrote *you* and *me* on the board, then asked the children, "How many words did I just write?" With enthusiasm the group responded, "Five!" (I was impressed with both the quick counting and the confusion about the meaning of *word* and *letter*.)

At another time, I had been invited to observe in a classroom occupied by four- and five-year-olds who were being prepared for reading. It was early in the year, and the teacher was working on visual discrimination. On the day of the visit, she had placed word cards in the slots of a chart and was asking individuals in a small group to find any two words that were the same. (Earlier work had concentrated on smaller combinations of letters, beginning with comparisons of just two.) All went well until the teacher pointed to a card displaying *Monday* and asked if anyone could find the same word on the chalkboard. At the start of the morning, *Monday* and *October* had been written, identified, and discussed. Now, in contrast with the earlier work, nobody could find it. Upon reflection, the children's failure to respond was no longer surprising—although at the time it was because of the earlier success. *Monday* had been printed on the board in large, white letters, whereas much smaller letters in black appeared on the card. What these children still needed to learn was the meaning of *same* and *different* applied to words. Eventually, they needed to learn that to all of the following, the same response must be given: flag, FLAG, flag , and *flag* .

Confusion over the meaning of taken-for-granted terms also caused problems in a first grade. In this instance, a student teacher had been asked to work with a boy who, unlike his classmates, had problems remembering the names of letters. Following a procedure she had seen the teacher use, the student teacher had arranged a row of letter cards and was asking the boy questions like, "This letter is *t*. What letter comes before *t*? . . . This letter is *c*. What's the name of the letter that's after *c?*" One had to conclude that the child really did need special help, for the number of incorrect answers matched the number of questions about the array of letters. As it happened, however, the student teacher eventually asked a different kind of question. She inquired, "Do you know what I mean when I say 'before' and 'after'?" The boy didn't, so the teacher wisely changed to a different procedure that had her point to a letter and ask, "What's the name of this letter?" Now, although not all answers were correct, many were. In another first grade, some of the children were busy with a workbook page, the directions for which had been, "Draw a line over all the pictures that . . ." In response, some were drawing lines above certain pictures and others were drawing lines through them.

Misunderstandings like those revealed during visits to classrooms are receiving attention in articles and research reports (2, 4, 12, 13, 20). In one, entitled "Component Skills in Beginning Reading," Calfee and Venezky describe an experience that is as pertinent for teachers as it is for researchers:

> Although many children use the words *same* and *different* . . . , their interpretation of these terms . . . may be different from the experimenter's. The writers ran headlong into this problem early in their testing program when one of the children replied "different" when shown two cards containing identical geometrical forms. When asked to justify his answer, the child pointed out that one of the cards had a smudge on it. With older or more test-sophisticated children, it is easier to communicate the dimensions with regard to which identity is to be judged. With younger children . . . the relevant dimension may be extremely difficult for the child to interpret. [2, p. 107]

Just how complex the language of instruction can be is also underscored in some observations made by Sticht et al.

> It seems likely that many children who are being taught to read may not know what they are to look for and focus upon, and may therefore have difficulty in learning to read. . . . For instance, suppose the teacher says, "Look at the word 'cat' on the blackboard." The child must aud the message, comprehend what a word is, understand that the utterance "cat" is a word in the spoken language, direct the gaze to the blackboard, visually examine the printed configuration and somehow understand that all three letters—not just "c" and "t" or "c" and "a" —are important elements of the graphic display of the spoken word "cat."
>
> The foregoing is quite different from the child's ordinary looking which is subservient to the child's self-imposed cognitive task. The teacher-imposed task may completely bewilder the child, making looking an almost pointless activity. This may be especially important if the teacher at one time expects the child to focus on whole words and at other times on elements of words. . . . A type of looking confusion could result, in that the child would not precisely know where to direct his focal attention. [20, p. 62]

Although of immediate importance, the meanings of words that figure in instruction are not something that is best taught in a given lesson on a given day. Instead, they come to be understood most precisely in a gradual way that is enhanced with many, many examples. While these understandings are growing, teachers of beginners need to bear in mind that when wrong answers occur, they may be rooted in confusion about the language of instruction.

Some terms that are often used in reading instruction are listed below.

word	line	beginning	next to
letter	under	first	top line
beside	before	last	last row
alike	after	front	first letter
different	end	below	same as

LANGUAGE EXPERIENCE MATERIALS

Narrowly defined, *language experience materials* are children's written accounts of their experiences told in their own language. As realized in classrooms, the term expands considerably to encompass any written material, long or short, that deals with in-school or out-of-school experiences of children in a given classroom. In many instances, the children's own words make up the account; in others, the words are similar but not identical. In still other cases, the words are a teacher's. The critical element is that the content pertains to a particular group of children —or to one certain individual. All other details (e.g., Should the teacher do the composing? Should a child's words ever be altered?) are determined by the reason for using the material. And this brings the discussion right back to a point underscored in an earlier chapter: *What* is done and *how* it is done ought to be determined by the reason for doing it—that is, by the instructional goal.

REALIZING BEGINNING GOALS
WITH LANGUAGE EXPERIENCE MATERIALS

What needs to be done to ease children into reading was listed on pages 96–97. Some of the things that language experience materials do especially well are listed below.* By comparing the two lists, you will see that they are closely similar.

SOME OF THE THINGS THAT CAN BE ACCOMPLISHED WITH LANGUAGE EXPERIENCE MATERIALS

1. Motivate children to want to learn to read
2. Personalize instruction
3. Demonstrate the connection between spoken and written language
4. Demonstrate the left-to-right, top-to-bottom orientation of written English
5. Demonstrate that the end of a line does not always mean the end of a thought
6. Demonstrate the value of written language for preserving information, ideas, and feelings
7. Teach the meaning of *word* and the function of space in establishing word boundaries
8. Teach the function of capitalization and punctuation

* How language experience materials function beyond the beginning stage is discussed in a subsequent chapter.

As is true of all instructional materials, those called "language experience" are a means for achieving one or more instructional goals. For that reason, the following accounts of how language experience materials can be used with beginners start with statements of goals. (The illustrations are not meant to suggest that a single lesson or experience clinches things. Typically—especially with slower children—repetition in some form is a requirement for understanding and retention.)

To Show the Connection between Spoken and Written Language.   By the time children arrive in school, they have learned language but they have not learned *about* language. One of the many things not understood by many is that what is said can be written. No better material exists to promote that understanding than written accounts of what the children themselves say. That is why a teacher might ask, "Who would like to tell us something that happened yesterday when you weren't in school?" and why she would print on a chalkboard lines like the following, even though some do not relate to her request. (As words are printed, they are read back to the children.)

Billy: I cut my leg yesterday.

Patricia: A fire engine woke me up last night.

Bobby: I'm going to go to my cousin's house after school.

At another time, children can be encouraged to say something about a picture they've drawn; then, as they watch, a teacher or aide prints and reads aloud exactly what they said. (See Figure 4–2 for examples of what nursery school children had to say about their pictures.)

One-word traffic signs can also demonstrate that written language is not as strange and mysterious as it might at first appear to be. Prior to the initial outdoor walk, a teacher might show signs attached to two long sticks. One sign displays *stop* (printed in lowercase letters since they are common in printed matter), and the other displays *go*. After identifying the two words (and then giving the children a chance to "read" them), the teacher explains that she will hold up *stop* whenever there is the need to stop walking, and the *go* sign when everyone can begin again. (Although this procedure originated in the teacher's desire to show the connection between spoken and written words, *stop* and *go* will end up in the reading vocabularies of some children. This is another example, then, of offering *opportunities* to learn to read.)

To Teach What "Word" Means and to Show the Function of Space in Establishing Word Boundaries.   Reading instruction, especially at the beginning, highlights individual words in a way that is foreign to spoken language. With the latter, one word flows into the next so rapidly that what is heard is a stream of sounds, not a series of distinctly separate words. This is why some children arrive

Figure 4–2. What Two Nursery School Children Said about Their Pictures

in school not knowing what *word* means and certainly not knowing that in print, empty spaces show where one word ends and the next begins. Experience material that is as short as two words can help such children.

To illustrate, let's say it's a very foggy Tuesday, so a kindergarten teacher decides to use the children's interest in fog to begin to give meaning to *word*. (As you'll see, what is done will also give the children the chance to learn to read *fog*, although that is not the central goal.) Following the children's interesting comments about the foggy morning, the teacher adds a few of her own: "You certainly know lots about fog, don't you? Let me show you what the word *fog* looks like when I write it. . . . This is what the word *fog* looks like when it's written."

On the next foggy morning, the same teacher might decide to repeat what was just described but to add to it, too. Thus the next time she might say after printing *fog* on the board, "Since you've been in kindergarten, you've certainly told me lots of interesting things about a foggy day. Let me show you what those two words, *foggy day,* look like when I write them. . . . This word [pointing to *foggy*] says 'foggy.' Did you see how I moved my hand over before I wrote the next word, the word *day?* I left an empty space so that you could see that I was writing two words, not just one. What do these two words say?" (Points to each as children read, "foggy day.")

For another illustration, let's say it is the fall of the year and the children have been out collecting leaves. Back in the classroom, their teacher gathers the group together to examine and discuss the collections. Leading questions about the leaves are posed periodically—for instance, "What colors are they?" "How do they feel?" "Are they all the same shape?" "How can we use them?" "What can we now say about our leaves?" Group contributions eventually lead to a written account, printed on the board by the teacher.*

> Leaves are different colors.
> Some are red.
> Some are more than one color.
> We're going to put our leaves
> in bottles.

The following guidelines are pertinent for the teacher who chooses to use this material to teach children what *word* means.

---

* Sometimes, what is written on the board should be transferred to chart paper so that when children eventually become more skilled in reading it can serve not only as practice material but also as evidence of their progress. Even if the children can't read the sentences, they can take a copy home to share with parents.

GUIDELINES FOR USING LANGUAGE EXPERIENCE
MATERIALS TO TEACH THE MEANING OF "WORD"

1. Say each word as you print it.

2. Read the entire account in a natural speaking fashion, pointing to each word as it is read.

3. Suggest to the children that they might like to read it, too. (As the children "read," read along with them, all the while moving your hand across each line of text from left to right.)

4. Point to and identify words that appear more than once. *If the children seem interested,* let them "read" these words.

5. Make a comment like, "There are so many words up here!" Then count them, pointing to each one. Show how a space separates one word from another. Next, let the children count the words. Point to each as it is counted.

6. Reread the entire account. Encourage the children to read along with you.

In addition to specifying what a word is and indicating the function of space to show word boundaries, the language experience activity just described (a) demonstrated that words are read from left to right and that lines are read from top to bottom; (b) pointed out that identical words look alike when they are written; (c) gave the children a chance to pretend they could read; and (d) gave them the opportunity to learn to read some words.

If the group had been fairly small or if the help of an aide had been available, the teacher might also have asked each child for his favorite word in the account. Named words could be printed on small cards to be taken home so that they could be read to parents and anyone else willing to listen. And so, reading vocabularies continue to grow.

To Demonstrate the Value of Print for Preserving Information.   Presumably, teachers everywhere are constantly demonstrating to children the literary contribution of written material by reading to them at least once every day from carefully chosen books. Language experience material is useful in demonstrating another contribution: it preserves information, thoughts, and feelings. To show the value of written records, a teacher might elect to use language experience material in the following way. (Remember, *how* it is used depends on *why* it is being used.)

Let's say for purposes of illustration that each school day in a certain classroom starts with a discussion of the weather, a topic of considerable interest to children, since it affects their play life. One Monday morning the teacher comments, "This certainly is a beautiful morning, isn't it? Was last Monday as nice as it is today? Can someone tell us what it was like last Monday?" Responses begin with guessing and end with the conclusion that nobody remembers. Thus it is time for the teacher to propose, "If I were to write some words that tell us what this Monday is like, then next Monday we could look at what I write, and it would tell us. We wouldn't have to work so hard trying to remember." A discussion of current weather then begins and leads to the printing of *sunny* and *clear* by the teacher at the left side of a very wide sheet of paper. By the end of the week, the sheet shows:

Monday	*Tuesday*	*Wednesday*	*Thursday*	*Friday*
sunny	cloudy	cold	rainy	sunny
clear	warm	dark	windy	clear
		windy		

A couple of weeks later, the teacher makes another proposal. "We seem to use the same words over and over, don't we? [Points to and reads *sunny, cold, windy,* and so on.] If I were to put these words on cards, then instead of writing them every day I could just pick out the right cards." Soon, a weather chart with slots for cards is attached to a bulletin board. Meanwhile, all the children work hard at remembering what each card says so that they will be able to select appropriate descriptions. And so, reading vocabularies expand still more.

TEACHER AIDES

Before the chapter ends, teacher aides need to be discussed because the help they can offer should not be taken lightly by any teacher whose target is individualized instruction. When classes are large, as a matter of fact, an absence of extra help can be one of the greatest obstacles to achieving excellence in an instructional program. Here I have in mind the teachers who are keenly aware of what individual children do and do not know and are knowledgeable enough to be able to select appropriate instruction, yet cannot execute their plans the way they would like to because there just aren't enough hands, eyes, and heads to go around. It is in situations like this that a second adult can make substantial contributions. Well prepared, she or he can be the difference between an ordinary program and a superior one. But, it has to be emphasized, the potential for that superiority must be in the teacher's plans. Otherwise, all an aide will do is contribute to mediocrity.

To illustrate this important point, I'd like to refer to a recent observation in a nursery-school class in which I found not one aide but two. When I arrived, the twenty children were distributed among three tables, each with an adult. One group was working on dittoed sheets that had them copying various geometrical shapes; another group was coloring a dittoed picture of a clown; those at the third table were arranging small sticks into piles according to their colors. Conversation was not encouraged; in fact, the children said surprisingly little while I was there.

Approximately twenty minutes after I arrived, the same three jobs were reassigned. The children who had been copying shapes were switched to coloring; those who had been coloring worked with the sticks; and those who had been sorting sticks received a copy of the geometrical shapes. After another twenty minutes, the same assignments were rotated once more.

For contrast, let me mention a kindergarten class where there was a teacher, an aide, and twenty-seven children. Thanks to the aide, the teacher was able to spend uninterrupted time teaching individuals and small groups what was important but unknown. Meanwhile, the aide did many things: answered children's questions; offered reminders to some; re-explained and checked assignments; read to a small group; discussed pictures with two children; listened to others read brief sentences that were on cards; wrote captions for children's art work; helped with spelling; demonstrated how to make certain letters. Clearly apparent was teamwork that began with a teacher who knew what needed to be done to achieve individualized instruction, and who was lucky enough to have an assistant who allowed her to do just that—without interruptions.

Because what needs to be done depends upon the children who are to be helped, an aide's responsibilities will vary from one situation to another. In all instances, however, it is important that aides know exactly what they are to do.

Some of the responsibilities that I have seen aides carrying out effectively are described below.

Direct Practice and Review.   When certain children require practice (its details would be determined by the teacher), an aide might supervise or direct it. If the practice involves games, the aide would play them with the children. If an entire class needs the same practice—printing certain letters, for instance—both the aide and the teacher might move about the room, examining work, making suggestions, and offering encouragement. In some instances, an aide is able to assume the role of tutor, offering assistance to individual children who need more explanations and practice than most. I have also seen aides who were especially helpful when children returned to school after being away for one or more days. Inevitably, absentees need varying amounts of help in catching up.

The most important point about all these possible roles for aides is that they assume only those for which they have the necessary ability and knowledge and that, for each role, they know exactly what they are and are not to do. This means that teachers must take the time to learn about their aides' abilities, add to them if necessary, and assign only those roles in which they can function successfully. The next step is helping the assistants grow in self-confidence.

Assist with Materials.   Among a teacher's many responsibilities is making certain that necessary materials and supplies are available, and at the right time. An aide can help with this by making sure materials are returned to the proper place, by keeping track of supplies and ordering what is needed, by duplicating ditto sheets selected by the teacher, and so on. Often, homemade materials will figure in instruction. While it is the teacher who must decide on their details, an aide can help make them. Here I am reminded of a first grade in which the teacher was full of good ideas for materials but lacked the ability to execute many of them. Her aide, on the other hand, had a great deal of artistic ability; so, together, this pair was able to produce some of the most attractive—and productive—materials I have ever seen. Once again, the teamwork was excellent.

Guide Conversations and Read Stories.   Once children know something, they want to talk about it. Yet in classrooms with many children but only one adult, opportunities for conversation are scarce. An aide can help with this, too, either by guiding a planned group conversation or simply by being available when a child just has to tell something to somebody.

Occasionally, an aide might also be the one who reads to the children. Or, as a way of accommodating special interests, a teacher might choose to read one story while the aide reads another. Dividing responsibilities this way also allows more children to discuss a story, once it has been read.

Help with Clerical Duties.   To visit regularly in classrooms is to be reminded of the many things a teacher has to do that hardly come under the heading of "instruction." Teachers still have to count money for milk, money for lunches, money for bus service, money for school pictures, and money for outings. They also must turn in attendance data, record test scores, and make out report cards. In one kindergarten, a teacher even had to keep track of which children were brushing their teeth with a fluoride preparation.

When a teacher has one group of children, extras like these are very time consuming; when she has two, they become a nuisance. They also take considerable amounts of time away from mornings and afternoons that are already too short to accomplish all that needs to be done. Clearly, an aide can help with many of the clerical duties now performed by people who should be given every chance to carry out their professional responsibilities. Without that assistance, teachers have to spend far too much time with matters that have little to do with education.

A SUMMARY

This chapter is the first of three that tell what can be done in pre–first grade programs both to prepare children for reading and to teach reading itself. For both goals, a language arts focus was recommended; reasons for the recommendation were cited in the chapter.

Since the readiness of pre–first graders inevitably varies, the chapter pointed out that instructional programs need to be assembled in ways that accommodate slow children like Paul (referred to in Chapter 3) and challenge bright children like Mary Anne. If this is to be accomplished, schedules must be such as to allow a teacher to spend time with individuals and small groups. One schedule that does that was discussed. How aides can help bring about appropriate instruction was considered, too.

Because all instruction must aim toward, and be guided by, specific goals, the chapter listed those that are especially relevant for reading at the very beginning. Even though some pre–first graders are beyond the beginning, early goals were identified in order to help teachers of unready children know what the important prerequisites for success are.

How to teach some of the prerequisites was illustrated in the chapter. Particularly emphasized was the value of language experience materials both to reach certain objectives and to make instruction personally interesting for the children. Attending to whatever is of interest is vital, since involvement and achievement go together.

The two chapters that come next will present additional features of instructional programs for young children. Together, the three chapters should paint a fairly complete picture of what can be done to foster ability in reading and, equally important, positive attitudes toward school and toward learning.

REVIEW

1. Facts presented in Chapter 4 include the following:
   (a) Young children are very interested in their own names.
   (b) Young children are often confused by the language that enters into reading instruction.

   Describe how first names can be used to teach children the meaning of "beginning of a word."

2. Working with a group of eight, a kindergarten teacher printed *red* on the board, told the eight what it said, then had them read it. Next she asked, "Can you think of anything that is red?" One child soon named red fire trucks, which resulted in an animated discussion of fires, fire fighters, and so on. Calling the group's attention back to *red,* the teacher pointed to it and asked, "What does this say?" Immediately the children responded, "Red fire trucks!"
   (a) Based on the children's response, what do they need to learn?
   (b) With specificity, describe what the teacher can do to teach what is needed.

3. Repetition is a natural part of songs. Repetition (practice) also is a requirement for word learning. Keeping these two facts in mind, select a song that would be of interest to young children; then describe how it might function in getting reading vocabularies started. The description should be sufficiently specific that your suggestions could be carried out in a classroom. (See Chapter 4 for suggestions related to "Old MacDonald.")

4. Let's say you are a kindergarten teacher who happens to have some old telephones, thanks to a telephone company. What type of Telephone Center can be organized to help with goals related to listening, speaking, reading, and writing? Specifically, describe some activities that would help with one or more of the language arts.

REFERENCES

1. Barrett, Thomas C. "The Relationship between Measures of Pre-Reading Visual Discrimination and First Grade Achievement: A Review of the Literature." *Reading Research Quarterly* I (Fall, 1965), 51–76.
2. Calfee, R. C., and Venezky, R. L. "Component Skills in Beginning Reading." In *Psycholinguistics and the Teaching of Reading,* ed. K. S. Goodman and J. T. Fleming. Newark, Del.: International Reading Association, 1969.
3. Criscuolo, Nicholas P. "Training Tutors Effectively." *Reading Teacher* XXV (November, 1971), 157–159.
4. Cutts, Warren G. "Does the Teacher Really Matter?" *Reading Teacher* XXVIII (February, 1975), 449–452.
5. Durkin, Dolores. *Children Who Read Early.* New York: Teachers College Press, 1966.
6. Durkin, Dolores. "Facts about Pre-First Grade Reading." In *The Kindergarten Child and Reading,* ed. Lloyd O. Ollila. Newark, Del.: International Reading Association, 1977.
7. Durkin, Dolores. "A Language Arts Program for Pre-First Grade Children: Two-Year Achievement Report." *Reading Research Quarterly* V (Summer, 1970), 534–565.
8. Durkin, Dolores. "A Six Year Study of Children Who Learned to Read in School at the Age of Four." *Reading Research Quarterly* X, no. 1 (1974–1975), 9–61.
9. Dykstra, Robert. "Auditory Discrimination and Beginning Reading Achievement. *Reading Research Quarterly* I (Spring, 1966), 5–34.
10. Hall, Mary Anne. *Teaching Reading as a Language Experience.* Columbus, Ohio: Charles E. Merrill Publishing Co., 1976.
11. Harris, Albert J. "Practical Applications of Reading Research." *Reading Teacher* XXIX (March, 1976), 559–565.
12. Holden, M. H., and MacGinitie, W. H. "Children's Conceptions of Word Bound-

aries in Speech and Print." *Journal of Educational Psychology* LXIII (December, 1972), 551–557.

13. Meltzer, Nancy S., and Herse, Robert. "Word Boundaries as Seen by First Graders." *Journal of Reading Behavior* I (Summer, 1969), 3–14.

14. Nurss, Joanne R. "The Schedule: Organizing for Individual Instruction." In *The Kindergarten Child and Reading,* ed. Lloyd O. Ollila. Newark, Del.: International Reading Association, 1977.

15. Paradis, Edward E. "The Appropriateness of Visual Discrimination Exercises in Reading Readiness Materials." *Journal of Educational Research* LXVII (February, 1974), 276–278.

16. Pikulski, John. "Readiness for Reading: A Practical Approach." *Language Arts* LV (February, 1978), 192–197.

17. Raim, Joan. "Rolling Out the Welcome Mat to Tutors." *Reading Teacher* XXVI (April, 1973), 696–701.

18. Robb, Mel H. *Teacher Assistants.* Columbus, Ohio: Charles E. Merrill Publishing Co., 1969.

19. Stauffer, Russell G. *The Language-Experience Approach to the Teaching of Reading.* New York: Harper & Row, 1970.

20. Sticht, T. G.; Beck, L. J.; Hauke, R. N.; Kleiman, G. M.; and James, J. H. *Auding and Reading.* Alexandria, Va.: Human Resources Research Organization, 1974.

CHAPTER

5

Helping with Language

PREVIEW

Several years ago, I heard a kindergarten teacher say, "I don't think we should do anything with reading. The kids aren't ready. I think we need to give more help with oral language. Let first-grade teachers take care of the reading."

While nobody can dispute the basic importance of oral language for reading, other thoughts are worth considering. For instance:

1. Might this teacher's objection to kindergarten reading stem from a concept of instruction that views it as coming directly from workbooks and ditto sheets? If this is the case, she *should* reject it.
2. Is it likely that *every* five-year-old is unready for reading?
3. Is this teacher's stand rooted as much in her own insecurity about teaching reading as it is in the conviction that kindergartners aren't ready?
4. If she does have an instructional program that provides interesting experiences and many opportunities to grow in oral language, wouldn't it only be natural to give a little attention to print, too? For instance, if the children are learning about colors and have enjoyed making one color from others, isn't it a natural next step to have the following on a bulletin board?

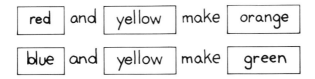

Chapter 5 is in this book to show how helping children with language can include procedures that *ease* them into reading.

Helping young children become competent language users has many dimensions. The one chosen for this chapter is the teaching of word meanings, which are viewed as being the product of knowledge acquisition and concept development. Underlying the chapter, therefore, is the notion that language allows children to communicate what they understand.

That children often use words when understandings are limited or confused is well known. A kindergarten teacher reminds us of this when she recalls how quickly her children named an anchor upon seeing a picture of a ship; yet, "when questioned about the function of an anchor, individual children said it was used to catch big fish, drag things out of the ocean, clean the bay, stop the ship, start the ship, catch crabs" (15, pp. 18–19).

Teachers always have to be on guard lest they become more concerned about naming than about understanding. Research reveals, for example, that in the middle- and upper-grades, a great deal of empty verbalization goes on in connection with subjects like social studies (7). Witness one conversation in a fourth grade:

Teacher: Who can tell us what a continent is?

Child: A really big place with states and countries and stuff.

Teacher: Could anybody give us another description?

Child: It's a large land mass.

Teacher: Fine. Good.

I wonder if this teacher would accept a first grader's concept of "happy" as being, "If your family goes to Pizza Hut, that's happy!" I hope so.

WORD MEANINGS AND READING

Just as a story is more than a list of sentences, so is a sentence more than a list of words. What a sentence is, in fact, is a series of words that relate to one another in ways that yield meaning. How relationships affect meaning is demonstrated in sentences like the following:

If you don't have space, get a folding table.

We could use a folding table in the laundry room.

The significance of relationships for meaning is also illustrated in the sentences below, which effectively demonstrate that a "simple" word like *see* is not so simple after all.

I see them over there.

See to it that nothing gets lost.

Please see to the children while I'm at the store.

Do you see the point he's trying to make?

She'll see them in her office at 3:15 tomorrow.

The bishop's see is a large one, isn't it?

They're trying to see what the problem is.

All the men will soon see service overseas.

Let me see you to the front door.

Let me see, how many more meanings are there?

Even though the meaning of a word often gets defined as it relates to other words and, second, even though the meaning of a sentence does not come from adding up the meaning of each word that composes it, it still must be recognized that knowing the meaning of lots of words is important for reading. To illustrate, can *you* read (read = comprehend) the sentence, "They are experienced spelunkers"? If not, a safe prediction is that the problem lies with the meaning of spelunker. (A spelunker, by the way, is one who explores caves.)

Just as common sense suggests that word meanings are important for reading, so too do research data (3). Repeatedly, vocabulary knowledge shows up as one of the most significant contributors to comprehension ability. Although teachers would be quick to agree with the findings of research on this point, what is done with word meanings in classrooms does not always reflect their importance. As children move through the grades, for example, a common procedure for dealing with vocabulary is reflected in an assignment seen recently on a fifth-grade chalkboard:

1. Write each word three times.

2. Look up its meaning in the dictionary.

3. Write that meaning.

4. Write a sentence using each word.

Although it is to teachers of young children that this chapter is addressed, any teacher reading it should be able to learn about ways for enlarging listening-speaking (oral) vocabularies that are superior to the practice just referred to.

CLASSROOM ATMOSPHERE

Providing the right atmosphere is hardly sufficient to equip children with oral vocabularies that will serve them well, both academically and personally; yet the classroom climate established by a teacher cannot go undiscussed. It either hastens language development or gets in the way; it is never neutral. One experience pinpoints the most important thing to be said about classroom climates. You might note a ring of familiarity about the details.

During a social gathering of a group of adults, a teacher was the last to arrive. When one of the other guests learned what her occupation was, he quickly commented, "Oh, I had better watch what I say." Although spoken in jest, his remark is relevant here in its implied reference to the tendency of a few teachers to be too quick to correct language. While the eagerness stems from a desire to improve it, constant correction is not likely to accomplish that end, because children soon learn to stop talking when whatever they say seems to be wrong. And children who do not talk do not learn to talk well.

Because teachers *are* responsible for improving language, they can hardly adopt an I-don't-care policy. If neither this nor constant correction is the answer, what is?

From what I have observed, the best answer begins with teachers whose own language provides children with a model worthy of both admiration and imitation. This means they neither talk down to children nor talk over their heads. Probably the natural tendency of teachers of young children is toward the former; therefore, let me comment about that, again through a personal experience.

I was interviewing teachers for a kindergarten position and went to the home of one because illness in the family made it difficult for her to be away for the interview. What especially impressed me about this candidate was the way she talked to her two youngest children, both of whom were present during our conversation. Her choice of words seemed just right; they were neither unnecessarily difficult nor childishly simple. This, coupled with other qualifications, impressed me enough to recommend that she be hired.

The next time I saw this teacher was the following fall when I visited in her classroom. Naturally I was both surprised and disappointed to hear her converse with the kindergartners in a way that could only be described as talking down. I cannot explain why she changed from a most acceptable way of communicating with young children; however, I can urge other teachers to avoid following her example because, first, talking down is unnecessary and, second, it deprives children of the chance to reach up to a language that, if imitated, will improve their own.

In addition to the language model provided by teachers, another relevant factor in creating the right atmosphere is their general attitude toward words. Ideally (again because attitudes are so readily picked up by young children), they should be enthusiastically interested in words. I say this not because research data support such a statement (studies dealing with this have not been done) but because classroom observations continually show that children's responses to words mirror that of their teacher. Find an interested teacher, I learned, and you will also find interested children.

More difficult to verbalize is still another feature of the ideal atmosphere. Here I have in mind what a teacher communicates to children about her role and responsibilities in relation to *their* language. What ought to be communicated is acceptance combined with a desire to help. Such a message has its beginnings in certain understandings about young children and language—for instance, that they must be encouraged to use it and that, essentially, they learn to use it well through trial and error. While it is somewhat difficult to describe this message in the abstract, in practice it looks very different from "You are wrong. I am here to correct you." It also is different in what it can accomplish.

WHICH WORDS TO TEACH

What can be accomplished when word meanings are the concern is affected by such variables as the ability of the children and the state of their existing vocabularies. As was mentioned earlier, the teachers' interest and their own facility with language are of considerable relevance, too.

While these and still other factors (e.g., insufficient time in a half-day program) may place limits on possible accomplishments, the words that can be selected for attention are *limitless*. With young children, as a matter of fact, the options are so numerous that the problem is not finding something to teach but, rather, deciding what to select from all that might be taught. That is why it always is surprising to hear teachers ask, "But what would I teach?" when they are being urged to give attention to word meanings. I can recall one in particular who was so ill at ease with the prospect of making plans for extending oral vocabularies that she said she could do nothing until she found a book that would help. Yet, on the very day she expressed the anxiety, she taught a song about a brook and read a story about a duckling.

What teachers need to remember is that everyday things and everyday happenings offer an abundance of possible subject matter. Searching for words—in a teacher's manual, for instance—is unnecessary, for looking at something as common and near as a shoe offers possibilities such as *pair, size, sole, heel, tongue, arch, lace, buckle, strap, leather, canvas, rubber, oxford, sandal, moccasin, tight, loose, comfortable,* and *uncomfortable.* A collection of buttons can help specify the meanings of *round, square, global, simple, ornate, cloth, plastic, bone, metal,* and *shell.* And I once watched as a teacher successfully used balloons not only to review color identification but also to give meaning to *stretch* and *inflate.* Although not every teacher will want to use shoes, buttons, or balloons, they do exemplify the ease with which subject matter can be found in the most commonplace objects. They also indicate that commercial materials are unnecessary.

Because of the abundance of possibilities, certain criteria can serve as guidelines in making word selections. Usefulness suggests that esoteric or seasonal words (*cornucopia,* for instance) should not be among the first to get attention. Difficulty is still another factor to consider—nouns, for example, are easier than qualifying terms, which are generally simpler than relational words (e.g., *on, be-low*). While all types are important, starting with what is easiest usually is the best procedure, since it promotes success and, in turn, self-confidence. Here it is important to point out that what might seem like a simple word can, in fact, be difficult (9). A goal like "Teach the difference in meaning between *look* and *see,*" for instance, is not an appropriate one for young children.

Children's backgrounds also bear on selections and, in many ways, overlap with another criterion; namely, the children's interests. With young ones, the great interest is themselves. Consequently, a demonstration of the meaning of *pair* should make use of *their* eyes, eyebrows, ears, cheeks, shoulders, arms, elbows, thumbs, legs, ankles, shoes, gloves, and stockings. Another common interest is what is already somewhat familiar. This means that what is close at hand and occurring in the present is what captures their attention.

In theory, it is easy to list criteria for selecting words, but in practice they are not clearly distinct. For that reason it is difficult to make statements about the relative importance of each. Were such a judgment required, I would list the criteria for making selections in the following order:

1. Children's interests
2. Children's backgrounds
3. Usefulness of word
4. Difficulty of word

PLANNED VERSUS UNPLANNED INSTRUCTION

While this book is a very open supporter (and promoter) of careful planning, no assumption is being made that it *automatically* results in successful instruction with word meanings. Let me describe just one in a long list of classroom observations that helps explain why this is the case.

The visit was in a first grade, and I was there at the teacher's request. She wanted me to see, and react to, one of her initial attempts to extend listening-speaking vocabularies. The attempt I witnessed focused on *happy* and *joy*. (The selection of an adjective and a noun created problems that became apparent when the children later suggested sentences using the two words.) The method chosen to teach the meaning of *joy* (*happy* was already familiar) was a mini-lecture to which the children responded with little interest, except for a boy who insisted that *joy* was the name of soap.

As it happened, I remained in the room for the rest of the afternoon and was glad I did because of what occurred during art. It was fall, so leaves were to be traced. In preparation, the teacher distributed a real leaf to each child—enough to create noticeable excitement. The children were encouraged to feel it, and as they did, the teacher talked about its veins and theirs, and also about the stem. But all this was done quickly in order to get to the tracing.

Since I knew this teacher was genuinely interested in helping with word meanings, I was naturally surprised that the potential in the art work was overlooked. Because it was, only a few of the children probably acquired new words for their vocabularies (*vein, stem, trace, outline*) when, in fact, an opportunity was available to teach them to all the children because all were so interested in the leaves.

As a result of this and other observations, several reminders assume importance for instruction in word meanings. The first is that *regular* instruction is necessary. Even simple resolutions like "I'm going to teach a word every day" or "I'm going to highlight one new word each week" are helpful. When instruction *is* scheduled, careful planning should precede it and ought to reflect awareness that young children are most responsive and interested when instructional procedures involve them in some active way. The lecture method, therefore, cannot be expected to win and keep their attention.

Another reminder is that opportunities to teach word meanings often occur in connection with other activities—for instance, with art. Teaching them at those times may be of greater interest to the children and, in addition, may be more meaningful. Because of the basic importance of vocabularies, the potential of these opportunities should always be utilized.

Still another reminder is that sometimes things just happen, either in school or out of school, which suddenly present a wonderful chance to teach meanings. Again, teachers should be flexible enough to take advantage of this.

In summary, then, three means are available for extending listening-speaking vocabularies:

1. Through regularly scheduled instruction
2. In connection with the achievement of other goals
3. Through unexpected happenings

SOME INSTRUCTIONAL PROCEDURES

This discussion of instruction with word meanings begins with accounts by teachers of some of the things they planned for the purpose of enhancing listening-speaking vocabularies. (They were prepared following the instruction.) While reading the accounts (Table 5–1), notice the variety of procedures that were used—also, how the children were actively involved. Notice, too, the importance of pictures for word meanings, which suggests that teachers ought to have

(*Text is continued on page 126*)

Table 5–1. Some Ways for Adding to Children's
Listening-Speaking Vocabularies

GOALS	PROCEDURES
To teach the meaning of fall and autumn. To introduce sequence of seasons.*	1. Used first day of autumn to introduce fall. Wrote it on board and pronounced it. Mentioned names of other seasons too. Also talked about different meanings of fall with help of sentences like, "Don't fall off your chair" and "Try not to fall when you play." 2. On the following day, introduced autumn as a word that can be used in place of fall. Read a story about the fall as a time of changing colors in leaves. 3. The next day took children to the park to collect leaves. Upon return to school, used them to remention fall and autumn and to provide practice in counting and in naming colors. (Learned children are confused both about colors and about counting. Future instructional plans will give attention to both.) 4. A week later, read story about squirrels gathering nuts to prepare for

* The teacher chose the second goal because of an answer from one of her more sophisticated kindergartners. Asked, "When does spring come?" the child responded, "In the fall."

Table 5–1. (Continued)

GOALS	PROCEDURES
	winter. (Also showed children some nuts.) Used story to review <u>fall</u> and <u>autumn</u> and to introduce the fall season as one that is followed by winter. Also mentioned that summer comes before fall. Showed this sequence with time line.
To call attention to words related to homes: <u>door</u>, <u>window</u>, <u>stairs</u>, <u>porch</u>, <u>roof</u>, <u>chimney</u>, <u>TV</u> <u>antenna</u>, <u>gutter</u>, <u>rain</u> <u>pipe</u>. To call attention to names of materials from which homes are often built: <u>wood</u>, <u>brick</u>, <u>stone</u>.	1. Used magazine pictures to name parts of house. Discussed reasons for chimney, gutter, and rain pipe. 2. Children drew pictures of their own homes or apartment buildings. 3. The next day, children were taken for a walk to look at different parts of houses. 4. The following day, story about a wooden house was read. Explained that other houses may be brick or stone. 5. After the story, children were taken for a walk to find wood, brick, and stone buildings.
To give meaning to <u>measure</u>, <u>ruler</u>, and <u>inch</u>.	1. Introduced measurement by asking, "If I wanted to know how tall you were, how could I find out?" This led to idea of measuring. Tape measure used to demonstrate how child might be measured. The word <u>inch</u> was intro-

GOALS	PROCEDURES
	duced. It was printed on the board; under it, a one-inch line was drawn. Then used a 12-inch ruler to measure length of comb, pencil, and sheet of paper.
	2. Later, reviewed measure, ruler, and inch by demonstrating measurement of toy car. Distributed sheets on which simple dittoed outlines of a comb, pencil, straw, and crayon were drawn. Children were to measure each and write the number of inches it measured beside the picture. (Comb was measured with much guidance to make sure children understood the task. Major problem: tendency to put ruler to edge of paper rather than to edge of picture being measured.) When measuring was completed, answers were checked.
	3. For several weeks afterwards, rulers were kept in a box on a table. Whenever there was free time, children could measure various objects in the room.
To teach the meaning of: orchestra, orchestra leader, baton, violin, trumpet, flute, trombone, clarinet, saxophone.	1. Once children were accustomed to their own band instruments, used pictures of orchestral instruments to introduce

Table 5–1. (Continued)

GOALS	PROCEDURES
	them to names of others. During three-week period, gave attention to each with the help of pictures and a musical recording that highlighted it. Summarized with bulletin-board display of labeled pictures.
	2. High school orchestra leader visited classroom bringing with him students who played the instruments that had been discussed. Each played a brief selection. The leader also explained and demonstrated use of the baton.
	3. Children visited high school when orchestra was practicing. One selection was played especially for them. Upon returning to the classroom, children played their own selections with the help of triangles, sticks, bells, and tambourines.
To teach names of baby animals: <u>calf</u>, <u>colt</u>, <u>chick</u>, <u>piglet</u>, <u>duckling</u>.	1. Showed picture of a woman holding a baby. Talked about it, mentioning that animals have babies too and that each has a special name. Talked about the familiar names <u>puppy</u> and <u>kitten</u>. Read a story that named and told about other baby

GOALS	PROCEDURES
	animals. Discussed each picture and counted the number of animals shown. Repeated their names.
	2. Prepared bulletin-board display of animals, each labeled. Talked about pictures to introduce art project, which was to make clay figures of a mother animal and her baby. Later, each was labeled and put on a table for display.
	3. Periodically, read a story about each animal that had been discussed. Later, to provide a review, reread story used to introduce the baby animal terms.
To teach the concept <u>circle</u>.	1. Began by asking, "Who knows what a circle is?" Showed circular objects: bracelet, clock face, penny, button, jar cover. Printed <u>circle</u> on board, identified it, then showed children a small paper circle on which the word <u>circle</u> had been printed. Said each would receive a circle to take home, to serve as a reminder to look for circular objects or pictures of them. The next day these were discussed.
	2. For the day circular objects and pictures were to be discussed, prepared

Table 5–1. (Continued)

GOALS	PROCEDURES
	bulletin-board display showing paper circles of different sizes and colors. Each was labeled <u>circle</u>. Used display for practice in counting and in naming colors and, with the help of questions and paper squares, to teach that the concept <u>circle</u> encompasses variation in size and color, but not shape.
	3. For the next day's art project, children were given paper circles of different sizes and colors, which were to be pasted on black paper to make a design.
	4. Pictures of circular objects brought in earlier by the children were assembled in a scrapbook cut in the shape of a circle. Each page was shown to them. Later, it was added to the collection of books that children can select at free-choice time. (Similar procedures were used to teach the concepts rectangle, triangle, and square.)

a large collection of all kinds of pictures, preferably large and colorful. The same accounts also point up the value of reading to children and of bulletin-board displays. What they do not show, on the other hand, is any need for manuals or other commercial materials.

Some remarks about the illustrative procedures shown in Table 5–1 follow:

1. Like all instruction, teaching word meanings *begins* with the selection of specific goals. In this case, goals are appropriate if they deal with words whose meanings are unfamilar but not overly abstract or obscure.

2. Sometimes other goals can be achieved with the same instruction. When *fall* and *autumn* were the concern, attention went to counting and identifying colors. Goals related to meanings also provided many opportunities to expose the children to written words, thus giving them the chance to learn to read them.

3. Selection of instructional procedures must consider their prerequisites. If children are not able to identify numerals, for example, they are not ready to use rulers to measure.

4. Selection of instructional procedures should also reflect use of the familiar to get to the less familiar. This was illustrated when *puppy* and *kitten* were introduced prior to terms like *calf* and *duckling*.

5. Generally, combinations of teaching procedures are used to realize a goal. Combinations in the illustrations included use of explanations, discussions, objects, stories, recordings, pictures, walks, and bulletin-board displays.

6. Even with young children, word study can make use of homonyms— for instance, *fall*. Homonyms are words that are spelled and pronounced the same but have different meanings.

7. Teaching word meanings is not to be confined to a specified period. In the illustrations, for example, time set aside for art was used to reinforce the attention given earlier to names of baby animals.

OTHER WAYS TO TEACH WORD MEANINGS

As the accounts of instructional procedures demonstrated, a great many ways exist to teach word meanings. The following pages single out those that are especially suitable for work with young children.* Some were mentioned in the accounts; now they will receive explicit and detailed attention. They include teaching through conversations, through question-answer sessions, through experiences, with visual aids, by reading to children, and in subject matter areas.

Because of the importance of talking for vocabulary development, that will be discussed first, initially under the heading of conversation.

---

* Procedures that are appropriate throughout all the elementary school grades are described in *Teaching Them to Read* (6).

Teaching Meanings through Conversations

In visiting classrooms, great contrasts are found when the amount of child talk is noted. In some, keeping silence almost seems to be the teacher's greatest concern; in others, the amount of constant noise seems intolerable. Somewhere in between, I would like to suggest, lies the teacher attitude about talking that is just right for young children in school. The hope is that by the end of this discussion, its details and standards will have been communicated.

To begin, it must be recognized that children in school—whether young or old—cannot be allowed to talk all the time, nor is it possible to let them talk whenever they feel like talking. Still, within the limits imposed by factors such as large classes, many opportunities should exist for young children to express themselves orally. In fact, there *must* be, because of the importance of talk for language development.

One such opportunity can be a conversation period—ideally, scheduled at the beginning of a day, since that is when children are most eager to talk both to the teacher and to other children. (A schedule that included time for conversation was discussed in Chapter 4.) When a teacher aide is present, arranging for conversation groups is no problem. The class can be divided into two groups so that each includes an adult and not so many children as to make conversation impossible.

When an aide is not available, arrangements are always less desirable, but conversation is still feasible. For instance, a teacher might choose to converse with one group of children while another is busy with something else. After about fifteen minutes, the groups exchange activities. With this kind of arrangement— particularly when it is a nursery school or kindergarten class—conversation periods cannot be scheduled as soon as the school year begins because the children first have to learn that there are times when they must busy themselves with something while the teacher is occupied with something else. For this reason, the suggestion must be: *Just as soon as possible* include a regularly scheduled time (not necessarily daily) for conversation.

Certain guidelines are helpful in carrying on a conversation. One is to keep it informal. Sitting around a table and avoiding (if possible) the requirement of raising hands often helps with this. Another guideline is that teacher talk should be *minimal* because the essential role of the teacher is to listen and, when necessary, to clarify or supplement.

Typically, when conversation groups first get underway the children seem shy, and many are reluctant to talk. At that time, the adult may have to ask a question, make a comment, or show a picture. Something like a large picture of children accompanied by questions (Who's in this picture? What are they doing? What do you suppose they'll do next? Have you ever done that?) can be counted on to get talk started.

As time passes, a different problem often develops—everyone wants to talk at once. Ideally, this problem should be turned into an opportunity to help the children understand that only one can talk at a time and that all will get a turn—should all want one. Obviously, no child should ever be obligated to talk, just as no child should be allowed to talk all the time.

In theory, it might seem desirable to use conversation as a time to teach the importance of staying with a topic and of making only relevant comments. In practice, such a goal is undesirable because attempts to achieve it inhibit the very thing that is to be encouraged—talk. And when children talk, there will be much that seems irrelevant.

When I first began listening to children's conversations, I assumed that the irrelevance reflected their age. But then I listened somewhat analytically to adult conversations and quickly learned that they were more like than different from those of young children. Participants commonly said what was of interest to themselves, whether or not it related to what had just been said by another. Often, in fact, it was as if each one was waiting to have his or her turn and merely tolerated what others were saying. This concentration on self suggests that teachers should not try to get from children what is uncommon among adults. Thus, they should expect to hear about many unrelated topics, even in a brief amount of time.

Occasionally, interesting connections between topics will be apparent. I recall one conversation in which a discussion about encyclopedias being big books prompted one child to tell the others about the big bruise on his leg. Much more often, however, topics will be many and varied and will bear little relationship—or at least not any that is obvious and certain—to one another. Exemplifying their winding course are some that were covered during one morning's conversation in a kindergarten:

> picture of harp shown by teacher
> Batman
> birthday party
> spot on the table
> men building a bridge
> acquisition of real horse
> chocolate milk
> television cartoons
> cows are not for riding
> clean fingernails

When young children are the participants in a conversation, other characteristics are identifiable. Almost always, they will introduce their contributions with either "Guess what?" or "You know what?" Common, too, are speech hesitations and repetition of words. And sometimes, especially when their contributions are long ones, the speakers will almost seem to be gasping for breath as they mention one thing after another. Also to be expected are sentences whose construction is far from perfect. For all this, the desirable response is patience, acceptance, and attentiveness.

Other responses from adults should reflect their awareness that conversation time presents opportunities to teach or clarify word meanings. Consequently, if on a rainy morning a child mentions that her coat is reversible, it would be appropriate to ask, "Does everyone know what 'reversible' means?" This gives the teacher or aide a chance to repeat the word (and, possibly, to print it on the board) so that all hear its correct pronunciation. Answers or the lack of them might indicate that an explanation is required.

Although explaining one word with others is not the best procedure for young children, it does have to be used some of the time. Still, its shortcomings ought to be recognized:

> One difficulty with this procedure is the danger of relying on superficial verbalizations. Meanings that are clear to the teacher may be quite hazy to the child. Many of the classical boners are due to superficial and inadequate grasp of word meanings. It is not sufficient to tell a child that *frantic* means *wild,* or that *athletic* means *strong;* he may try to pick *frantic flowers* and pour *athletic vinegar* into a salad dressing. [11, p. 409]

One way to minimize superficial verbalizations is to let children have their say when words are being explained. What will be heard will be interesting. I recall being in one classroom when the teacher was explaining *freedom.* Among other things, she said that children are "not free to do bad things, such as take somebody else's coat." Immediately, one of the children objected with "Sometimes it's okay to take a coat. When you have company you say to them, 'May I take your coat?'"

Often, children's responses will be helpful for diagnostic purposes because they are so revealing. Misconceptions about age and time, for example, are common; thus it hardly comes as a surprise to hear a question like, "When you get to be a very old man, say about nineteen years old, does your body stop growing?" Nor is it surprising to get quite different definitions for a word like *manners* from two children with very dissimilar family backgrounds. Asked for its meaning, one child explained, "It's something you have to use very nicely when you use it," whereas the other said, "It's if you don't push anybody down and give them a bloody nose."

Other responses from children will reveal what they have been learning, which makes them highly rewarding for a teacher. Relevant here is a first-grade class in which a unit on "Helpful Animals" had been used to extend vocabularies. Among the animals studied was the lamb; especially highlighted was its double contribution of food and clothing. About a month after the unit ended, some of the children were talking about Christmas during a conversation period. Evidently the holiday reminded one child of lambs, which reminded another of woolen clothing. This soon led to a discussion about the frequency with which woolen mittens are given as Christmas presents. Such a conversation could have been nothing but satisfying for the teacher who was listening.

This would also be true for a kindergarten teacher who was giving help with the pledge to the flag. Each day she talked about the meaning of a word likely to be unfamiliar, beginning with *pledge* itself. Approximately one week after it had been discussed, she happened to say to a conversation group, "I brought a special picture to school today. Promise you won't look while I go get it." Quite agreeably one child commented, "I pledge *I* won't look!"

In another kindergarten, the teacher had read a story about frogs and gave some attention to the word *speckled* because of its frequent appearance in the story. Some of the illustrations helped by displaying its meaning. On a subsequent day, again at conversation time, she happened to show the children a large photograph of some new puppies, one of whom was dotted with spots. This time the rewarding response from a child was, "He's really speckled, isn't he?"

Teaching Meanings through Question-Answer Sessions

A somewhat structured procedure for encouraging talk is what might be called "question-answer sessions." These are suggested by the fact that if you want children to talk, you must give them something to talk about. If done well, such sessions foster thought as well as talk. For example, once children are accustomed to the question-answer technique, queries like these might be posed to a small group:

> What would happen if . . .
> > everyone forgot his or her name?
> > everyone sang a different song?
> > everyone fed the fish on the same day?
>
> What would you do if . . .
> > the clock at home stopped running?
> > the bus broke down on the way to school?
> > two pages in a book were stuck together?
>
> Tell me why . . .
> > I wore a coat today.
> > we go to school in the morning rather than at night.
> > people watch television.

With other questions, experimentation as well as discussion are in order. For instance:

> Are you taller when you stand up or when you lie down?
> Will a piece of ice melt faster outdoors or indoors?
> Is the water in the fish tank lower today because the fish drank it?

Used with pictures (or the objects themselves), the questions "Which go together?" and "Why?" can be productive. In this case, sets of pictures might show objects like:

> cup, glass, plate, bowl
>
> bird, boy, house, nest
>
> fence, house, door, gate

Deliberately, pictures would sometimes be combined in ways that promote conflicting answers and, as a result, group discussion.

The combination of pictures and questions also is helpful in teaching the meanings of *alike* and *different*. In this case the question is, "How are these alike and how are they different?" and it would be posed while the children were considering pairs of pictures that might show:

> vase, bottle
>
> mittens, gloves
>
> radio, television
>
> worm, snake
>
> large plain ball, small striped ball

Meanings of other pairs of words could also be taught with questions about pictures. Here I refer to combinations like:

> fat, thin
>
> wide, narrow
>
> close, far
>
> tall, short
>
> happy, sad
>
> full, empty
>
> dark, light
>
> heavy, light

A question, this time combined with demonstrations, can offer assistance with relational words. Using something as ordinary as buttons along with the question "Where is it now?" a teacher or child could demonstrate the meanings of such words as *under, over, between, next to, above,* and *beside*.

Depending on the children, it might also be possible to use questions like, "Could you hear this?" in connection with such statements as:

> An ant walking on dirt
>
> A fence running around a yard
>
> A clock telling time

Whatever the focus, the important thing to keep in mind when using question-answer sessions is the reasons for having them. The first is to encourage children to talk and thus to use the words they already know. The second is to teach them new ones. The third is to get them to respond in more thoughtful, analytical ways. All in all, the potential of question-answer sessions does make them something that should at least be tried.

Teaching Meanings through Experiences

I can think of no more effective way to communicate the importance of experiences for word meanings than to quote a passage from a textbook by Dolch:

> The average adult tries again and again to tell children with words what things are. . . . The child asks, "What is a snake?" The adult says, "An animal that crawls along the ground." The child imagines such an animal and asks, "But his legs will be in the way." The adult says, "Oh, he hasn't any legs." So the child takes off the legs and sees a legless body lying there. "But how does he crawl around without legs?" "He wiggles," says the adult. The child tries to make the legless body wiggle. "How does that get him to go forward?" The adult loses his temper. The peculiar way in which part of the snake pushes the other part cannot be described. It has to be seen. Let us go to the zoo. [5, p. 309]

The effectiveness of this quote might have one drawback. It could lead you to conclude that "providing children with experiences" means taking them on a trip or doing something exotic in the classroom. That is not the case, however. Should a selected goal be to give meaning to *pair,* teaching procedures might begin with a brief verbal explanation coupled with a reference to the children's shoes, eyes, ears, and so on. Following this, a procedure like the following could provide an experience to solidify its meaning:

- Fill two boxes with identical collections of small objects (e.g., earrings, dice, socks, bracelets, shoelaces, knitting needles). Have children take turns selecting an object from one of the boxes. Each child names his object, finds the same object in the second box, then places the two side by side on a table. The eventual result is a display of pairs of objects.

Experiences to help clarify the multiple meanings of *shade* might include on various days: (a) going outside to figure out why there is shade on sunny days;

(b) staying inside to examine a number of lampshades; and (c) coloring squares to illustrate shades of a given color.

That children should *expect* words to have more than a single meaning is important for reading. I was reminded of this while visiting in a third grade where the teacher was discussing a character in a story that the children had just read. With a series of questions, she was trying to get them to reach a conclusion about his behavior. Not succeeding, she commented, "He certainly was a patient person, wasn't he?" All agreed. Then she inquired, "What does the word *patient* mean?" One child explained, "It means when you're sick and you go to the doctor and he tells you that you have to go to the hospital."

Multiple meanings also were evident in a kindergarten classroom I like to visit because the teacher is always doing something interesting with words. Often, she brings experiences into school because large classes and no assistant make it difficult to go outside. For example, one morning she invited a police officer to speak to the children. Always careful about preparations, she had read a story about police in which the words *crest* (for the badge on their hat) and *uniform* were especially highlighted. She mentioned this to the visitor prior to his coming, so he used these words several times as he talked. And then an interesting thing happened in connection with his use of *crest*. It reminded a child of the name of her toothpaste which, of course, she mentioned. In turn, others named theirs. To the amusement of the adults (the children went right on naming brands), one boy said his toothpaste was "sex appeal."

This particular experience, in addition to reminding us that life with young children is never dull, offers other reminders too. One is that vocabularies are enlarged through experiences only if the growth is planned for. In fact, the richest experiences can be fruitless if a teacher does not see to it that certain words are selected and then given explicit attention—sometimes before, during, and following the experience.

This same point has been made very effectively by Frazier (8). He puts it this way:

> Experience may be said to have been fully experienced only when it has been worked through in terms of language. The meaning of experience has to be extracted, clarified, and codified, so to speak. Perhaps, then, one of our chief challenges in working more productively . . . with all children is to attend more carefully to the development of vocabulary from whatever experiences they are having. [8, p. 176]

Since experiences do have great potential for vocabulary development, it is important for teachers to keep in mind (this was exemplified in the police officer's visit) that elaborate ones are unnecessary. A walk through the community, for example, might be the best of dictionaries for *shingle, dormer, cupola, shutter,* and *eaves*—or, *rain pipe, gutter,* and *chimney.* A walk anywhere allows for scavenger hunts, which, in turn, can result in collaborative collages back in the classroom. Arrangements of items glued to a board in the order in which they were found allow for labels like *first, next, later* and *at the end*. Or, depending on what was found, neatly printed cards might display such descriptions as *small, smaller, smallest,* or *big, bigger, biggest*.

Seeing in the ordinary great possibilities for vocabularies is not the same as saying that special trips should never be taken. A trip to an airport, after all, is very effective in changing the meaning of *airplane* from a noisy spot in the sky to a structure of unexpected size, while a trip to the zoo can change *snake* from an unbelievable creature into something starkly simple. Probably the most generally useful reminder in this regard is that the productivity of an experience is not dependent upon its elaborateness or exotic quality, but upon what a teacher does to ensure that word meanings are clarified as a result of it.

Still another reminder is to be found in the description of the police officer's visit. It is important to make plans with the people who are involved in an experience. With the police officer, planning merely required asking him to talk about his uniform and, more specifically, the crest on his hat. With other resource people, preplanning may take different forms. Why some type is always necessary is explained well by a teacher:

The first year I taught I knew it was important to provide children with experiences, and I guess I assumed they would automatically result in better vocabularies. I remember very well the first trip I planned. It was to a greenhouse and, other than to get permission from the owner to come, I made no special preparation. The result was a tedious tour that seemed more appropriate for botanists than my first graders. It was sufficiently disappointing that we didn't do much more with trips for the rest of the year.

By my second year of teaching—thanks to some things I had read—I was more aware that the good that comes from excursions is not an accidental happening. What comes, I learned, must be planned for ahead of time. For that reason, at the start of the second year I spent some time with the florist before I took my new group to see his greenhouses. Because of the time we spent together, this second tour was most productive. It started by calling the children's attention to the printed word *greenhouse*. Many of them knew *green*, some recognized *house*, and all seemed to know why it was an appropriate name once we arrived at our destination. On this tour, the florist showed the children how all the plants were kept warm in winter and how each one was individually watered by a tiny hose connected to a larger one. At the end of the discussion, he turned on the entire sprinkling system. Need I mention how much this delighted the children?

They were also delighted when, at the end of the tour, each received a small bag of crocus bulbs. Earlier, the florist had demonstrated some planting and had shown pictures of what their bulbs would look like in the spring.

The end result of all of this, combined with some discussion and showing of pictures when we got back to school, was new or more specific meanings for *greenhouse, florist, sprinkle, hose, bulb, temperature, mum,* and *chrysanthemum*. (The connection between the last two words was brought out during the tour. At first the florist used *chrysanthemum,* then switched to *mum.* One of the boys picked this up immediately, commenting, "That's not what you called it before." Very nicely the florist explained the connection. Fortunately, when we got back to the room I remembered to write both on the board so that the children could see how *chrysanthemum* included *mum.*)

Encouraged by the successful trip to the greenhouse, this teacher followed it up with one to the post office. Out of class, preparations began by talking with the worker who was to be the guide; in class, by having the children compose a thank you letter to the florist. The teacher later typed it and showed and reread it to the children. She then addressed an envelope and stamped it, and off everyone went to the post office to mail the letter.

At the post office, the group was met by the guide. The tour itself began by dropping the letter in the "city" slot. It proceeded by tracing what would be done with the letter in order to get it to its destination.

Preparation for the next trip, this one to a firehouse, began when the children were taught to read *red.* During the discussion, fire trucks naturally were mentioned. This reference was followed by stories about fire trucks and fire fighters. Then it was time to ask the children, "Would you like to go to the firehouse some day?" They soon went and not only learned about a variety of equipment but also got to stand on the rear of the trucks. The climax came when the fire fighter who was acting as guide let all the sirens ring.

As it happened, the trip offered many opportunities not only for vocabulary development (*fireman, firehouse, fire truck, axe, pick, siren, ladder, hose*) but also for attention to other goals. While discussing the trip, the teacher wrote *red* and all the children identified it. She also wrote *fire* and then showed how it was part of *fireman* and *firehouse.* Because the children had already been introduced to the sound recorded by *f,* these same words were used to review that. Later, at art time, each child received a copy of a typed, two-sentence caption:

Look and see the boys and girls.

See the fire truck.

The children read the sentences, then drew pictures to go with them.

This trip and others (newspaper office, lumber yard, pharmacy, jewelry store, hatchery, grocery store) effectively demonstrate how different goals can be worked on simultaneously. This is an important point to remember because in talking or writing about teaching, only one thing can be mentioned at a time; consequently, it is possible to give the impression that a teacher does this *or* that—for instance, she works on word meanings *or* reading *or* phonics. What the descriptions of the trips correctly point out is that most of the time a teacher meshes goals and works on more than one. With the trip to the firehouse, for example, the selected goal was vocabulary development. Yet, in both the preparation and the follow-up periods, the children learned to read *red;* were exposed many times to *fire;* were introduced to compound words (*firehouse, fireman*); and reviewed what they had learned earlier about the sound that *f* stands for. Because teaching requires attention to numerous goals, it is a consolation to know that, often, more than one can be dealt with at the same time.

Teaching Meanings with Visual Aids

If clarifying one of the meanings of *shell* were an instructional goal, everyone would agree about the desirability of having the children see crustaceans in their natural habitat. Since that is possible only in rare cases, the next best experience would be a trip to an aquarium. If that, too, had to be ruled out, probably the next best thing would be an excursion on a beach to find empty shells; less desirable would be a collection of shells in the classroom. If even that was unavailable, another substitution would have to be used—pictures.

Although pictures and other visual aids are only substitutes for the real thing, they can make extensive contributions to vocabulary development if chosen with care. Some aids, of course, will be more helpful than others. Photographs, slides, and films, for instance, typically are better than drawings. And colored photographs, slides, and films generally are more effective than those in black and white. Even the best of aids will be productive, however, only to the extent that they are used with forethought.

The word or concept selected for attention also has something to do with how effective any visual aid will be. For example, *square* can be pictured more accurately than *cube,* and *circle* is easier to portray than *globe*. In fact, three-dimensional objects always suffer, leading to the tale of the urban child who, when seeing a cow for the first time, was amazed to find it was not flat.

Other children, subjects in a study of lower socioeconomic groups, had great difficulty interpreting stylized illustrations (14). Shell-like blossoms on a hilly background, for example, were thought to be a turtle. Other misinterpretations led the researcher to conclude:

> It could be inferred from the findings of this study that teachers . . . need to pay particular attention to the selection of visual stimuli used to extend experiences, to build concepts, and to enlarge vocabularies. Unless such pictures are extremely realistic, the experiential impoverishment of disadvantaged children may lead to difficulties. [14, p. 224]

On the positive side, carefully selected visual aids help with what at first might appear to be nonpicturable meanings. The material in Figure 5–1, for instance, shows how a picture can display meanings of relational words. (Suggested by the material, too, is the possibility of making picture dictionaries to help with word meanings and, later, with alphabetical order.) I have also been in classrooms in which scrapbook collections of magazine pictures communicated very

From *My Picture Dictionary*, by Hale C. Reid and Helen W. Crane, of the GINN ELEMENTARY ENGLISH series, © Copyright, 1963, by Ginn and Company (Xerox Corporation). Used with Permission.

Figure 5–1. Using Pictures to Help with Word Meanings

Knowing the precise meaning of relational words is important for reading, which makes pictures like the one above highly useful. Pictures such as this also suggest classroom activities. For instance, if up and down are getting attention, children can be asked to name whatever comes to mind when they think of up and down. Later, what is named—ladders, stairs, roller coasters, seesaws—can be drawn and labeled "up and down."

effectively the meanings of words like *devotion, serenity,* and *anticipation.* Although being used with middle-grade children, the collections successfully demonstrated that pictures can pinpoint the meanings of abstract terms with an accuracy and even emotional overtone that cannot be matched by verbal explanations.

A classroom illustration will make one final point about pictures used with young children. In a first grade, the boys and girls had been divided into groups for conversation. On the morning of the visit, an aide was with the boys and the teacher was with the girls. The teacher had chosen to get things started by displaying a picture of a small girl holding a puppy. The group showed interest, but almost immediately one girl called attention to the pin she was wearing on her dress. From that point on, everyone talked about pins, apparently forgetting the picture of the girl with her puppy. This was no problem for the teacher, however. She simply used the unexpected interest to teach more about *pin.* She displayed the girl's pin. She also showed a straight pin and safety pin, and the children discussed their uses. Knowing that they could read *in,* the teacher printed that on the board and demonstrated how she could change it to *pin* by adding an initial *p.* Also being demonstrated was the productivity of instruction that is grounded both in flexibility and in an awareness of educationally significant goals.

Teaching Meanings by Reading to Children

It seems that nobody ever gets too old to enjoy a story. Visits to nursery school, kindergarten, and primary classes further suggest that the younger the person, the greater such enjoyment is. That is why it never ceases to be a delight to see a group of children become one—no matter what their differences in ability and behavior —as they listen with ears *and* eyes to a story. Occasionally, the interest will be less, but that usually happens when the wrong book is chosen.*

Reading to children serves a variety of significant purposes—so many, in fact, that it should *never* be omitted from a school program. As mentioned, it promotes enjoyment and, with it, positive feelings about books and about school. In addition, it can move nonreaders to want to become readers.

Especially valuable for children who speak nonstandard English is the contact with standard English that is provided each time somebody reads to them. (Nonstandard English and its significance for instructional programs is discussed later in the chapter.) Regardless of what their speech patterns are, however, all children stand to profit from the practice they are getting in comprehending written linguistic structures, which are somewhat different from those found in spoken language. Often, too, the information gleaned from listening will help with comprehension when the children are doing their own reading later on.

---

* If inexperience leaves you feeling insecure about choosing books, you can find help in items listed in the References at the end of the chapter (1, 13, 16, 19, 20). In one, for example, the author names and briefly describes books found especially suitable for young children (20). Another lists books and notes the concepts each teaches (1). Other good sources of help are children's librarians, available at most public libraries.

Not to be overlooked is that an effective presentation by a teacher or an aide provides children with a model of what good oral reading is. And certainly not to be forgotten is the value of reading for extending listening-speaking vocabularies. All in all, reading to children is hardly a minor activity.

BENEFITS OF READING TO CHILDREN SUMMARIZED

Fosters positive attitudes toward books and school

Motivates children to want to become readers themselves

Gives them opportunities to hear the syntactic patterns of literary language

Provides a model of good oral reading

Communicates information that will help with comprehension when they themselves read

Teaches concepts and word meanings

When concepts and word meanings are the concern, a variety of options is available for book selection. The most common procedure is to select one without consideration of this extra goal, thus with total concentration on the factor of enjoyment. This was what was done when a teacher who was mentioned earlier chose to read a book about frogs. As it happened, *speckled* was used frequently, and it was also explained well with pictures. Therefore, calling the children's attention to its meaning was natural and in no way interfered with enjoyment.

Sometimes, but less frequently, vocabulary development should play a more active role in book selection. This results in reading one that not only interests the children but also deals directly and fully with certain concepts. An example would be *Let's Find Out What's Big and What's Small* (see Figures 5–2 and 5–3). In a book like this, clarification of concepts and words is built into the content and illustrations; it is not "stuck on" as sometimes happens, nor is it preached. Having read it to many children, I know they enjoy it.

Other selections can be made from books that were explicitly written to help with concept development. Illustrative of these is a series, published by the Golden Press, called *First Adventures in Learning Program*. Probably the best way to describe this series, and thus suggest themes commonly found in others, is to list a few of its individual titles:

Listening for Sounds

Adventures with Color

Understanding Numbers

Time and Measuring

Next to an elephant, a rabbit looks small.

From *Let's Find Out What's Big and What's Small* by Martha and Charles Shapp, copyright 1959 by Franklin Watts, Inc. Reprinted with permission of Franklin Watts, Inc., p. 11.

Figure 5–2.

Next to a mouse, a rabbit looks big.

From *Let's Find Out What's Big and What's Small* by Martha and Charles Shapp, copyright 1959 by Franklin Watts, Inc. Reprinted with permission of Franklin Watts, Inc., p. 12.

Figure 5–3.

Discovering Shapes
Learning about Sizes
Adventure with Words

No matter how good the concept books might be—and quality varies greatly —young children usually are not as interested and involved as when they are being treated to a story. This suggests two guidelines. First, when a book is primarily concerned with concepts rather than characters and plot, it generally is a good practice to read only part of it at one sitting unless it is very short. Or to make this same point differently, do not expect the same attention span that is typical when a story is being read. And certainly never expect to get the response sometimes heard when an especially good tale has just ended—"Read it again, please."

The second suggestion is to read concept books to small groups rather than an entire class. This is wise because the small numbers allow for discussion and make it easier for children to look carefully at illustrations, which usually are an integral part of concept books (see Figure 5–4).

From DISCOVERING SHAPES by Tina Thoburn, copyright © 1970, 1963, p. 19. Reprinted with permission of The Bobbs-Merrill Co., Inc.

Figure 5–4.

Float and Sink

Some things float.

Some things sink.

Some things float and sink.

Things heavier than water sink.

Things lighter than water float.

Ice

1. We put water into the freezer.

2. The water is a liquid.

3. The water is freezing.

4. The water is a solid.

5. The water is ice.

Figure 5–5. A Summer School Science Program

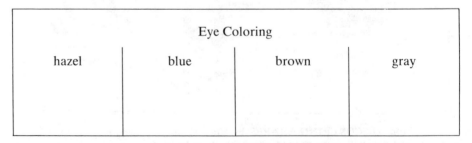

Eye Coloring

hazel	blue	brown	gray

Figure 5–6. Bulletin Board Display

Teaching Meanings in Subject Matter Areas

Both this chapter and the two preceding ones showed how music and art can be instrumental in readying young children for reading; in teaching them to read; and in extending their listening-speaking vocabularies. When listening-speaking vocabularies are the concern, subject matter areas like social studies and science should not be forgotten, because—at whatever level they're taught—both should enlarge children's understanding of themselves and their world; and one by-product of that understanding ought to be an enlargement of their vocabulary.

In pre–first grade programs, limited time and numerous goals typically eliminate daily attention to subjects like social studies and science. Nonetheless, both offer many ideas for productive activities that can be carried on whenever time permits. To illustrate, let me describe what one teacher did during a six-week summer session that was for children who would be entering kindergarten in the fall.

This teacher viewed the summer program as a time to ready the children for reading in ways similar to what was described in earlier chapters. She also saw the six weeks as offering an opportunity to use science experiments to extend listening-speaking vocabularies.

The first series of experiments focused on water. Although the unit began with water play, simple, carefully planned experiments were soon going on. A little of what was done with water is reflected in the homemade book shown in Figure 5–5. As a result of this unit, the children had the chance to learn the meaning of words like *liquid, freeze, solid, boil, steam, evaporate,* and *chill.* (Some learned to read these words, too.) The grand climax for the unit was a Kool-Aid party.

As an observer, I concluded that children in this program acquired lots of new information and words; equally important is that they were learning that going to school is a very desirable thing to do.

BULLETIN BOARDS

Throughout this chapter, materials that help advance children's vocabularies have been described. Noncommercial types received attention because what teachers put together themselves can match what children are interested in and what they need to learn.

Bulletin-board displays will be singled out here because they can be especially effective in synthesizing and summarizing. This is shown in a bulletin board seen during an observation in a first grade. Unfinished, the board looked like Figure 5–6.

During the observation in this first grade, the children were busy drawing and coloring pictures of their own faces, which were to be cut out and glued in the appropriate column on the bulletin board. The teacher mentioned that she often used activities like this one to call attention to word families. Therefore, another column was on the chalkboard; it displayed:

color

colors

colored

colorful

coloring

Descriptions of other bulletin-boards used to promote vocabulary development follow:

- In a kindergarten where there was an aide, the class divided into two groups to make cookies. Although each worked separately, preparations were the same: a simply composed recipe was listed on a large sheet of chart paper. With each group, the teacher (or aide) read the ingredients, giving particular attention to *teaspoon* and *tablespoon*. To help clarify their meanings, a teaspoon and tablespoon were shown, and the children talked about their uses. Later, while the children were enjoying the fruit of their labor, the teacher put one of the charts on a small bulletin board to which she also attached a teaspoon and tablespoon. Eventually, a fork and knife were displayed, after their uses had been discussed.

- Divided into four sections, a bulletin board in a kindergarten was called "Shades of Colors." Names of colors (blue, yellow, green, brown) provided titles for the sections. In each, the teacher had arranged rows of the small, plastic squares that decorators use to help customers select paint colors. This was highly effective in demonstrating that a word like *blue* hardly refers to one color.

- A kindergarten teacher had been working on the names of animals and their homes. To summarize, she prepared a bulletin board showing pictures of a cage, nest, bowl, stream, barn, jungle, cave, and pen. A pocket had been made at the bottom of each picture by stapling to it three sides of a rectangular piece of construction paper. The teacher also had a collection of animal pictures. The display was used by having individual children name an animal shown by the teacher. After it was identified, the child named its home and then placed the animal's picture in the correct pocket. (Later, playing with the display could be selected by any two children at free-choice time.)

- In another classroom, monthly bulletin boards were prepared. They were used each morning to teach the children to read the names of the months, to practice naming numerals and colors, and to teach word meanings. For April, the board showed a large tree in the background and flowers and bushes in the foreground. For use with this display, the teacher had cut out thirty tiny birds. Before the display was assembled, spring had been discussed in order to introduce *migrate,* a term used frequently during April. As each of its days passed, one bird was added to the board, attached either to the tree or to a bush. Daily, the birds were counted and *migrate* was mentioned. (Unexpectedly, the children became very interested in birds; consequently, April turned out to be a month for bird watching and naming. Books about birds were read, too.)

- One first-grade teacher had been giving attention to homophones. (Homophones are words that are pronounced the same but have different spellings and meanings.) They were introduced with a bulletin board showing two paper trees labeled, "A Pair of Pear Trees." At the start, a picture of a pear was pasted to one while the other held a picture of two shoes. Nothing more was done with the board while homophones were being taught, although the children did know that at some time they would fill up both trees with pictures. At the conclusion of the instruction, the bulletin board was used again, this time to summarize. Now the trees showed pictures depicting *one, won; sea, see; break, brake; blue, blew; Mary, merry.* (In this dialect area, *merry* and *Mary* were pronounced the same, thus were homophones. In some areas, their pronunciations are different.)

- In another classroom, a teacher used a similar procedure to introduce and summarize more work with homophones. It was October, so the bulletin-board theme was, "Which is Witch?" The board itself was divided into two sections. At the conclusion of the instruction, one part displayed pictures for *ate, aunt, red, meet, wee.* The other had pictures depicting *eight, ant, read, meat, we.**

Two concluding comments about bulletin-board displays are called for. First, because the written words on a board should look as much as possible like the words the children will see later in books, capital letters should be used as

---

* It happened that both teachers labeled the pictures displayed on the boards. This is one time, however, when I would not endorse labeling because for children who are either getting ready to read or are just beginning, the idea "sound alike but are spelled differently" might be an unnecessary source of confusion. It would be important that they realize the sounds of homophones are the same even though their meanings are different; but they need not be told *yet* that their spelling is different. This additional characteristic could be mentioned later, when reading ability is somewhat established and more homophones are being taught.

sparingly as they are in books. With titles, therefore, only the first letter in words should be capitalized.

The second comment is the reminder that bulletin-board displays should be placed sufficiently low that their details can be both seen and touched. If a teacher feels compelled to couple displays with warnings of "Do not touch," it is possible that she is one who should not have them—at least not if she teaches young children.

NONSTANDARD ENGLISH

A chapter that has highlighted the significance of oral language for success with reading cannot bypass the much discussed topic of nonstandard English. While such a topic has many dimensions, the one that is especially relevant here is the question, What effect does a child's nonstandard speech have on his or her efforts to become a reader of standard English? Not to be forgotten, however, is another equally important concern; namely, what effect do school expectations and attitudes have on the child with nonstandard speech?

Since *factual* answers for both questions are unavailable, all that will be done now is to point up some general guidelines and reminders for those who teach nonstandard speakers. Subsequent chapters will pinpoint more specific guidelines for certain aspects of reading instruction.

Deficit versus Difference

At one time, teachers were routinely told that any form of English that was not "standard" (generally defined as the type of English that is used by well-educated people and appears in such printed material as textbooks) had to be improved. Improvement meant "changed to standard English." In retrospect, this is known as the *deficit* view, for it assumed that nonstandard forms of English such as those listed below (22) are both inferior and deficient:

> Acadian English
> American Indian
> Hawaiian pidgin
> Northern urban black
> Southern Mountain (Appalachian)
> Southern rural (black and white)
> Spanish-American

For a number of reasons, recent years have witnessed changed attitudes toward nonstandard English. One is the research of linguists who, in analyzing various black dialects, have found that what was once thought to be deficient speech is in fact ordered on the basis of highly developed principles and rules (4, 18, 22). Compared with standard English, these dialects do show surface differences in vocabulary, pronunciations, and grammar. However, nothing is lacking for effective communication.

With such findings, another attitude toward nonstandard English has evolved. It is referred to as the *difference* view, which contends that differences do not constitute either deficiency or inferiority.

Implications for Teachers

Whether teachers hold to the deficit or the difference point of view, what was said earlier in the chapter is pertinent for classroom practices and expectations:

1. Children should be encouraged to talk.
2. What they say should not be subject to constant correction.
3. A teacher's own language ought to provide children with a model worthy of imitation.

In the context of nonstandard speech, what was said earlier about the importance of teachers' reading to children bears repeating, too:

1. Children should be read to at least once a day. (This is especially important for children who have not been read to at home.)
2. Reading aloud permits children to hear standard English, which is what all children have to learn to read.
3. Reading aloud to children gives them an opportunity to hear the syntactic patterns of literary language, which are different from those that characterize both standard and nonstandard speech.

For teachers who work with young children whose home language is some form of nonstandard English, still other reminders are important. Prominent among them is that the *primary* responsibility of the school is to teach children to read (comprehend) standard English. (Whether it can teach nonstandard speakers to *speak* standard English—which is an entirely different issue—is dependent upon many variables, most of which are not controlled by the school. Here, significant variables are family and peer-group expectations and attitudes, and, at later ages, vocational interests.) Acceptance of the primary responsibility regarding reading has some implications for teachers:

GUIDELINES FOR TEACHERS OF CHILDREN WHO SPEAK NONSTANDARD ENGLISH

1. Young children who speak nonstandard English should be given continuous opportunities to hear standard English as a preparation for the language they will encounter when they learn to read.

2. While nonstandard speakers are having such opportunities, nothing should be done or said that might suggest their own speech is inferior. (How people speak is an extension of themselves. To reject their speech is to reject them.)

3. When what young, nonstandard speakers say is written as a way of showing the connection between oral and written language, it should be put down and read back as spoken (e.g., "All the time he be sad"). When this is done, correct spellings should be used, again as a way of preparing the children for what they will have to deal with when they learn to read.

4. Once young, nonstandard speakers have some notion of what reading and print are all about, standard English should characterize written materials. This reflects the objective of instructional programs: to teach all children to read (comprehend) standard English.

A SUMMARY

Having dealt with many different aspects of vocabulary development in this chapter, let me now summarize some of the more important points.

To begin, the chapter was based on three assumptions. One is that language should be an asset for a child, not a liability. To ensure that it *is* the former, school programs must do whatever they can to extend children's listening-speaking vocabularies.

The second assumption of the chapter is that the development of listening-speaking vocabularies has nothing to do with tasks like memorizing dictionary definitions, but that it has *much* to do with experiences, knowledge acquisition, and concept development.

The third assumption is that listening-speaking vocabularies make substantial contributions to success with reading, which is why they are highly relevant for a book intended to help children learn to read.

Because young children's vocabularies are naturally limited, those who teach them should have no trouble finding words for instruction. To guide selections, four factors that ought to be considered were discussed. They include the interests and backgrounds of the children as well as the usefulness and difficulty of the words themselves.

Procedures for extending listening-speaking vocabularies were described and are listed below.

EXTENDING LISTENING-SPEAKING VOCABULARIES

Teach meanings:
   through conversations
   through question-answer sessions
   through experiences
   with visual aids
   by reading to children
   through subject matter areas

As the list indicates, there is a variety of ways to add to children's vocabularies. Nonetheless, the chapter repeatedly pointed out that even the best procedures—for example, providing children with experiences—will be productive for vocabularies only to the extent that teachers *plan* for them to be productive.

In the discussions of instructional possibilities, many references were made to materials. Homemade types were featured in the chapter because they can be assembled to match not only children's interests but also their vocabulary needs. As with all materials, those mentioned were viewed as being a means to an end—in this case, extending vocabularies.

The needs of nonstandard English speakers were discussed next. While everything said in the chapter applies equally to standard and nonstandard speakers, a few additional suggestions were made to those who work with the latter.

REVIEW

1. Chapter 5 illustrated how ordinary things (e.g. shoes, balloons) can help with word meanings. How might an orange or a pencil help?

2. Toward the end of the school year, a group of first-graders each assembled a word-meaning book. The first page in one child's book showed the neatly printed sentence *I am thin,* which she illustrated with labeled drawings of

string, a pin, a match, and a toothpick. What might another sentence be and what are appropriate drawings for it?

3. Let's say that you're a teacher and you've been organizing some of your work with vocabulary around the five senses. To summarize, you've prepared five boxes labeled *see, hear, feel, smell,* and *taste.* You're now collecting pictures, which will be sorted by the children and placed in the various boxes. Describe suitable pictures for this activity. Examples are given below to get you started.

see (sunset)   smell (perfume)
hear (bell)   taste (candy)
feel (porcupine)

4. Carefully planned lessons designed to achieve a given goal are not as common as they ought to be. One way to improve instruction is to provide lessons that will (a) achieve their end, and (b) be of interest to children.

Read a story that appears to be suitable for reading to four- to six-year-old children; as you do, look for words whose meanings might not be understood by the majority of this age group.

(a) List the words.

(b) Choose one word and describe an effective way of explaining its meaning(s).

REFERENCES

1. Adams, Ruth R., and Litwin, Zelda. "Talking Typewriter—A Study in Concept and Attention Growth of Young Children." *Elementary English* XLVII (February, 1970), 250–256.

2. Artley, A. Sterl. "Words, Words, Words." *Language Arts* LII (November/December, 1975), 1067–1072.

3. Davis, Frederick B. "Psychometric Research on Comprehension in Reading." *Reading Research Quarterly* VII (Summer, 1972), 628–678.

4. De Stefano, Johanna S. *Language, Society, and Education: A Profile of Black English.* Worthington, Ohio: Charles A. Jones Publishing Co., 1973.

5. Dolch, Edward W. *Psychology and Teaching of Reading.* Champaign, Ill.: Garrard Press, 1951.

6. Durkin, Dolores. *Teaching Them to Read.* 3rd ed. Boston: Allyn and Bacon, 1978.

7. Durkin, Dolores. "What Classroom Observations Reveal about Comprehension Instruction." *Reading Research Quarterly* XIV, no. 4 (1978–79), 481–533.

8. Frazier, Alexander. "Developing a Vocabulary of the Senses." *Elementary English* XLVII (February, 1970), 176–184.

9. Gentner, D. "Evidence for the Psychological Reality of Semantic Components:

The Verbs of Possession." In *Explorations in Cognition,* ed. D. A. Norman, D. E. Rumelhart, and the LNR Research Group. San Francisco: Freeman, 1975.

10. Golinkoff, Roberta M. "A Comparison of Reading Comprehension Processes in Good and Poor Comprehenders." *Reading Research Quarterly* XI, no. 4 (1975–76), 623–659.

11. Harris, Albert J. *How to Increase Reading Ability.* New York: Longmans, Green and Co., 1961.

12. Johnson, Dale D., and Pearson, P. David. *Teaching Reading Vocabulary.* New York: Holt, Rinehart and Winston, 1978.

13. McCormick, Sandra. "Choosing Books to Read to Preschool Children." *Language Arts* LIV (May, 1977), 543–548.

14. Morgan, A. L. "A New Orleans Oral Language Study." *Elementary English* LI (February, 1974), 222–229.

15. Robinson, V. B.; Strickland, D. S.; and Cullinan, B. "The Child: Ready or Not?" In *The Kindergarten Child and Reading,* ed. Lloyd O. Ollila. Newark, Del.: International Reading Association, 1977.

16. Root, S. *Adventuring with Books.* New York: Citation Press, 1973.

17. Shafer, Robert E. "The Work of Joan Tough: A Case Study in Applied Linguistics." *Language Arts* LV (March, 1978), 308–314.

18. Shuy, Roger W. "Some Considerations for Developing Beginning Reading Materials for Ghetto Children." *Journal of Reading Behavior* I (Spring, 1969), 33–43.

19. Sutherland, Zena. *The Best in Children's Books.* Chicago: University of Chicago Press, 1973.

20. Taylor, Marie E. "Instant Enrichment." *Elementary English* XLV (February, 1968), 228–232.

21. Tough, Joan. *Focus on Meaning: Talking to Some Purpose with Young Children.* London: George Allen and Unwin, 1973.

22. Venezky, Richard L. "Non-Standard Language and Reading." Working Paper No. 43. Madison: Wisconsin Research and Development Center for Cognitive Learning, 1970.

CHAPTER

6

Teaching Manuscript Writing

PREVIEW

If someone were to ask in what order the language arts develop in children, "Listening, speaking, reading, and writing" would be the usual response. While this sequence is common, it is not inevitable. Some of the children who arrive in kindergarten already reading, for example, learned to read *after* they learned manuscript writing (3, 6, 12, 15). In addition, an experimental school program for four- and five-year-olds (7) has shown that opportunities to print are more attractive to some children than any concerned with reading. Because of these findings, it is recommended that teachers of young children provide them with the chance (not the obligation) to learn to print. How to do that is the subject of Chapter 6.

Although Chapter 6 is called "Teaching Manuscript Writing," the instruction it covers can accomplish far more than the title suggests. More specifically, instruction with manuscript writing can be a vehicle for helping with visual discrimination; for teaching letter names; for demonstrating that words are composed of letters; for introducing and then reinforcing the fact that letters stand for sounds; for pointing out that the writing (spelling) of a word is related to its sound; and, finally, for teaching letter-sound associations.

As the multiple goals point up, the instruction described in Chapter 6 is concerned not only with manuscript writing but also with beginning phonics. As it touches the latter, it shows how the whole-class drill with phonics that is so common in beginning reading programs can be replaced with something that is not only more meaningful and productive but also more enjoyable for the children.

As you go through the chapter, you will find numerous ideas for instruction and practice. To make them more retrievable for your teaching, you might want to write each on an index card that can be filed in a box under some appropriate heading—for instance, "Practice with Initial Consonant Sounds."

Technically, printing is called *manuscript writing*. This contrasts with *cursive writing,* the type adults commonly use. That cursive writing is what they do use prompts a question about why schools teach manuscript writing first.

HISTORY OF WRITING INSTRUCTION

Early publications indicate that at the start of the century, cursive writing was taught to beginners; and at that time the question was, Why teach *any* kind of writing to six-year-olds? That was being asked for the same reasons reading for six-year-olds was being questioned. Since the reasons were discussed in some detail in Chapter 3, only a brief reference will be made to them now.

During the early years of this century, recapitulation theory was widely accepted. As a result, references to it were common in educational discussions, including those about writing. Patrick, for example, reminded his readers in an article published in 1899 that writing should never be taught before the age of ten because "it will demand a considerable maturity in the child before he is ready for that which has developed so late in the history of the race" (14, p. 390).

Further evidence of the influence of recapitulation theory appears in an article by Dewey published in 1898. In this case, he was criticizing both reading and writing instruction as he observed:

> There is an order in which sensory and motor centres develop—an order expressed, in a general way, by saying that the line of progress is from the larger, coarser adjustments having to do with the bodily system as a whole (those nearest the trunk of the body) to the finer and accurate adjustments having to do with the periphery and extremities of the organism. The oculist tells us that the vision of the child is essentially that of the savage; being adapted to seeing large and somewhat remote objects in the mass, not near-by objects in detail. [5, pp. 319–320]

The early years of the century were also marked by singular attention to the maturation process and to such related phenomena as neural ripening. It is not surprising, therefore, that educators of the times were also saying, "It is a well-known fact that a child's powers, whether physical or mental, ripen in a certain rather definite order" and "the child's mind, before ten, has not ripened sufficiently for tasks like reading and writing" (14, pp. 386–387).

Even though (as these various quotes point out) all writing instruction was being criticized and, secondly, even though the critics were well-known educators and psychologists, the change that eventually came about was one that merely replaced cursive with manuscript writing. Why?

While American educators were advocating the postponement of all writing, some in England were claiming that manuscript is easier than cursive writing and, therefore, should be taught to young children (9). The influence of English educators upon early childhood education was considerable at that time; thus it is not surprising that manuscript writing was imported to America in the early 1920s. Once here, it was used with gradually increasing frequency until it finally became routine to teach it to school beginners.

Why is manuscript writing easier for beginners? It is easier primarily because it is made up of letters that, in addition to being separated from one another in words, are themselves composed of separate strokes. Or, as another has put it: With manuscript writing, the child can "stop, rest, and get his bearings before making the next stroke or the next letter" (9).

Another reason often cited to explain why manuscript writing is taught initially is its close correspondence with the print found in beginning textbooks (11). The thinking here is that manuscript writing and text print go hand in hand, whereas use of the cursive type introduces differences at a time when everything should be done to simplify learning.

VISUAL DISCRIMINATION ABILITY

Because printing instruction gives careful, explicit attention to the shapes of letters, it helps with visual discrimination. Differences in children suggest, however, that not all will be ready for, or interested in, printing. Teaching visual discrimination apart from printing instruction, therefore, needs to be considered, since that ability is important for beginning reading.

For a teacher, the first question is *not* how to teach it. Rather, the first task is to learn whether such teaching is necessary. Children who are able to name letters, for instance, hardly need help, since letter-naming ability is evidence of visual discrimination ability. (How to learn whether children can name letters—and colors and numbers—was discussed in Chapter 4.)

For children who can neither name letters nor see differences among them, work with visual discrimination begins with attention to two letters with obviously different shapes—for example, o and f. An appropriate question about them is, "Do these two letters [pointing to each] look the same, or are they different?" Eventually, the same question is posed about closely similar pairs. Meanwhile, written assignments can provide for practice.

Written assignments give children the chance to compare letters on their own and to make judgments about the shapes. For such exercises, letters should be typed in columns, not rows, because the former facilitates comparisons with the target letter—the one typed (preferably with a primer-size typewriter) at the top of the column. The child's job is to underline or circle all the letters in a column that look like (or are different from) the one at the top. No more than four or five letters should be in a column—again, to facilitate making comparisons.

Because work with visual discrimination is not an end in itself but is meant to help with reading, a shift to more than single letters should be made as soon as possible—to comparisons of *if* and *if* or of *if* and *ff,* for instance. Most of the time, letters for such comparisons should spell a word, since that allows for extra but important comments from a teacher: "Yes, these two letters [points to *if*] are just like those two letters [points to *if*]. These two spell the word that says 'if,' so those two letters spell the same word. *If* is a word that we use a lot. Sometimes you hear me say, 'If you are quiet, I'll be able to read this story.' "

Casually naming words reflects a recommendation that has been made many times before; namely, give children *opportunities* to learn to identify words. Casual naming can be surprisingly effective in building reading vocabularies—at least for some children.

LETTER-NAMING ABILITY

Nursery school and kindergarten teachers who offer instruction about the names of letters probably assume that letter-naming ability contributes to a child's success with beginning reading. This is an appropriate time to consider the assumption.

To do that, it is necessary to go back to 1958, when Donald Durrell published a series of studies that examined the correlation between an entering first-grader's ability to name letters and his later ability to learn words (8). These studies indicated that letter-naming ability was a better predictor of word learning than any of the other variables under investigation.

Although flaws in the Durrell research were soon identified in an article by Helen Robinson (17), the finding about letter-name knowledge received widespread attention, which was probably fostered by the earlier publication *Why Johnny Can't Read,* by Rudolph Flesch (10). In what turned into a best seller, Flesch laid the blame for reading problems on the school's use of whole word methodology (which discouraged attention to individual letters) and promoted in its place immediate instruction in phonics (which would highlight individual letters).

In subsequent years, other studies also reported high correlations between letter-name knowledge and success with beginning reading. Simultaneously, interest in teaching phonics was growing. One outcome was encouragement for publishers to include in their workbooks a large number of pages that concentrated on letters. Since what gets into workbooks gets into classrooms, it is not surprising to find that much time is now being spent on letter-naming exercises, sometimes as early as nursery school. What about this?

Certain points need to be made about the developments just described before specific comments are offered about the practice of teaching letter names to young children.

One is the reminder that the Durrell studies were conducted at a time when kindergarten programs were not teaching anything as "academic" as letter names. This suggests that the beginning first-graders who were tested in Durrell's research probably learned them from a non-school source. Why such children could be expected to be successful readers has been explained by Samuels:

> . . . the kind of home background which enables a child to enter first grade knowing many of the letters of the alphabet would be the kind of home in which academic achievement is stressed. . . . it is well known that socio-economic status and home environment are highly correlated with school achievement. [18, p. 72]

Another observation made by Samuels is valid whether young children learn the names of letters in school or at home:

> . . . learning to name letters of the alphabet is a paired-associate task and may be taken as an index of intelligence. Since we already know that in elementary school I.Q. is highly correlated with reading achievement, it is not surprising that letter-name knowledge is also correlated with reading achievement. [18, p. 72]

For this discussion, the most important point to make about correlation data—whether coming from studies concerned with letter naming or something else—is that they say nothing about cause-effect relationships. This means that even though achievement in one area (letter naming) commonly goes along with another (reading ability), it cannot be assumed that one accounts for the other. For teachers, it means that instruction in letter names will not necessarily cause children to be better readers.

Since this is so, should programs for young children give attention to letter naming? Two everyday observations, I believe, provide an answer. First, even though children who do not know letter names can learn to read, a knowledge of some (not necessarily all) facilitates reading instruction by allowing teachers to call attention to the distinctive features of words. ("This word is *doll*. It does look like *dog*, but it ends with *ll*, not *g*.") Letter naming will also figure in phonics instruction. ("All these words begin with the same letter, with *b*. If you listen as I read them, you'll hear that they begin with the same sound.")

One further reason for giving attention to letter names is rooted in the fact that, because of television programs like *Sesame Street,* many pre–first graders now arrive in school interested in letters and with a knowledge of at least some of their names. Why shouldn't nursery schools and kindergartens do whatever they can to extend both the interest and the knowledge? By doing so, they can ensure that the names of letters are firmly fixed in children's minds before attention shifts to their sounds. This will keep the children from confusing one with the other.

One way either to extend or to initiate a knowledge of letter names is to provide printing instruction. The following sections discuss its details.

BEGINNING PRINTING INSTRUCTION

The method of instruction to be described is recommended because it links print-ing with beginning reading skills, and because research demonstrates that it works (7). Even so, nothing in the recommendation suggests it is the best or the only method. In fact, the more I visit classrooms the more convinced I become that there is no such thing as one best way to teach anything. What is successful and of interest to some children can be either boring or frustrating for others. And a method that works well with one teacher seems doomed to immediate failure when used by another. What is described, therefore, is simply a way of teaching printing that you might want to consider for your own work with young children.

Initial Decisions

One of the first questions a teacher needs to answer about printing is which manu-script system to follow. Many are available from a wide variety of publishers; one sample is shown in Figure 6–1. Comparisons between this system and others show that differences are minimal and deal either with the shapes of a few letters or the direction in which some strokes are made.

Since research has nothing to say about which system is best, selections are usually made because of factors like familiarity and convenience. They also are commonly made by people other than the teacher; thus, you might find yourself using what has already been chosen. (If you are a nursery school teacher and are making the selection yourself, find out what system is used in the local schools, because choosing the same one allows for continuity.)

Regardless of how the decision is made, the important thing for teachers is that they have some system and that they use it with facility. (The same directive is relevant for parents, which suggests the wisdom of providing them with a copy of whatever system is used in school. At a pre-school meeting for parents of pros-pective kindergartners they could be taught how to print and could also be re-minded that lowercase letters are far more important than the capital forms.)

Once a particular way of printing letters has been chosen, the next decision has to do with the sequence for teaching them and with whether the capital and lowercase forms of each letter will be presented together or separately.* When writing workbooks are used, both questions already have answers—assuming a teacher chooses to use them exactly as they are assembled. When this is not the case, or when workbooks are either unavailable or bypassed, a teacher does need to give some thought to sequence. To help, a number of criteria will be mentioned.

---

* The terms *capital* and *lowercase* (not *small* and *big*) should be used with children for the simple reason that some "small" letters are as big as capital letters.

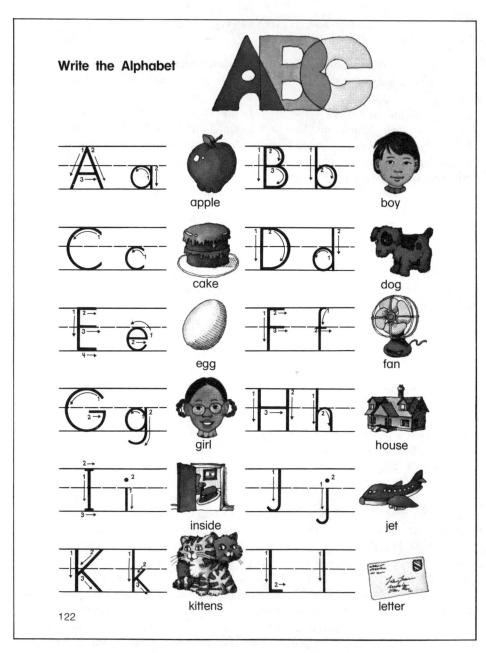

Write the Alphabet

apple

boy

cake

dog

egg

fan

girl

house

inside

jet

kittens

letter

122

From *Language 1* of the GINN LANGUAGE PROGRAM, © Copyright, 1979, by Ginn and Company (Xerox Corporation). Used with permission.

Figure 6–1.

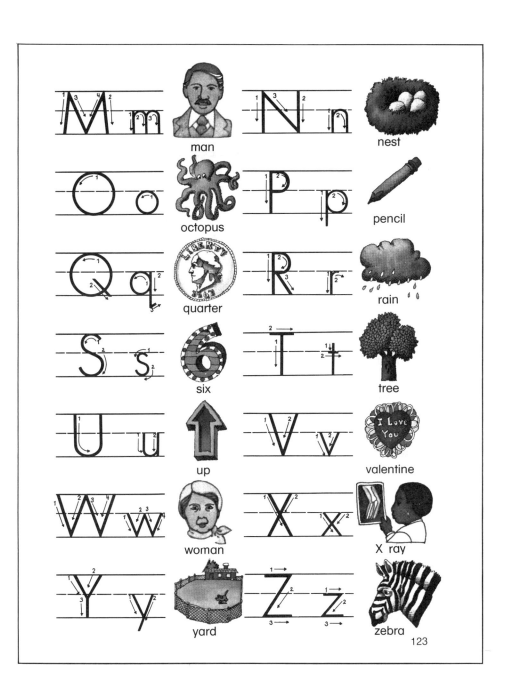

man

nest

octopus

pencil

quarter

rain

six

tree

up

valentine

woman

X ray

yard

zebra

123

One is difficulty. This suggests starting with the more easily made letters such as *i, l, t,* or *x.* Mentioning *x* leads to another criterion: usefulness. Because writing letters is a means to an end—the end in this case being ability to write words—attention to less frequently used letters like *x, q,* and *z* should be postponed.

Likelihood of confusion is another consideration. Here the notorious problem with *b* and *d* comes immediately to mind, suggesting that attention to each be separated by time. The same guideline applies to pairs like *p* and *q.*

The last criterion to be mentioned is, in my opinion, the most important. I refer to interest and the observable fact that some letters are more appealing than others. Those in a child's name, for example, always are special for him, but others can be made special. I recall a nursery school class in which the letter *s,* often difficult to make, presented no problems when introduced on the day that brought winter's first snow.

What kind of paper to use is another practical concern. At the start, when children's efforts result more in scribbling than in writing, large unlined paper can be used. Soon, though, a shift should be made to manuscript paper, which has uniformly spaced lines that make demands pertaining to placement and size. (If children print on chalkboards, they should be lined, too.) For manuscript writing, paper is placed squarely in front of the child with its lower edge parallel to the edge of the desk or table; the child's nonwriting hand is placed at the top to keep it from moving. It goes without saying that nothing should be done to try to change the left-handed writer.

In the beginning, help should be given in how to hold a pencil correctly: between the thumb and first finger, resting on the others. Even though earlier decades had much to say about the need for oversize pencils with young children (this was one outgrowth of the exaggerated attention given maturation) observation indicates they are awkward—not easier—to handle. Thus, regular-size pencils should be available. They ought to be reasonably long, which is to say *not* like the stubs that are so frequently seen when classrooms are visited.*

One other question about printing has to do with the pace of instruction. Here, the only sensible guideline is to teach the letters as quickly as the children are *comfortably* able to learn them—but no faster. What turns out to be a comfortable pace will be affected not only by the children's age, motor coordination, and interest, but also by the amount of time allotted to printing instruction. In a nursery school—should the teacher decide to have some writing—it might be as limited as one or two weekly periods of about fifteen minutes' duration. In first grade, on the other hand, it would probably be daily periods of varying lengths.

---

* A finding from the research with preschool readers that was referred to earlier is relevant here. The children routinely used regular pencils before starting school; then, in first grade, they were given extra large ones because official school policy said they were unready for the regular size (6). Isn't it unfortunate that we pay such slight attention to children when we make decisions or issue proclamations about them?

Getting Ready for Printing

Whether you teach (or plan to teach) nursery school, kindergarten, or first grade, remember that individual children might have done some printing before coming to school. For the most part, they will only know about capital letters (unless their parents were informed about the importance of lowercase letters) and often will be using incorrect strokes. Nonetheless, they *have* begun and usually do not require the basic preparation that is essential for others.

The others often have to learn such basic things as how to hold a pencil and how to keep paper from moving. They may also need to learn referents for *top* and *bottom* and for *left side* and *right side*. If their experiences at home did not include the chance to use pencils, crayons, and paper, they'll also need to do some scribbling in order to get a feel for the materials and to experience "pencil power." Once it is experienced and some control is achieved, the scribbling can be channeled somewhat. I recall one kindergarten teacher who, by having children color the spaces resulting from a limited amount of scribbling, turned their papers into interesting mosaics—or as one child aptly described them, "windows like my church has."

Following the aimless scribbling, beginners should next be encouraged to try to copy or make objects. Of special relevance for printing are round or oval shapes such as are found in wheels, doughnuts, pumpkins, snowmen, eyes, and eggs. Straight lines also are important and can be practiced when children make doors, windows, fences, ladders, and so on.

Thus far, attention has gone to physical preparations, but this is not meant to overshadow the psychological, for getting children *interested* in learning to write is of major importance, too. Some, of course, already have the interest. They have watched parents or perhaps older siblings write at home; now they want to learn. When the interest has not been acquired, probably the quickest way to foster it is to entice the children with the prospect of learning to print their names, always a perennial favorite not only with the young but, as Dale Carnegie tells it, with adults, too (2).

Finding occasions to call attention to names is no problem. The combination of a teacher's taking attendance (done with cards held by her) and signing first names to the children's papers and possessions (e.g., crayon boxes and coat hooks) is enough to highlight them. Before long, the children will want to print their names themselves; thus, it isn't long either before instruction can get under way.

Potential of Printing Instruction

All instruction, whether with printing or with something else, ought to aim toward clearly defined objectives. Therefore, let me introduce this discussion of printing lessons by mentioning the goals they can *eventually* attain:

WHAT PRINTING INSTRUCTION
CAN ACCOMPLISH FOR CHILDREN

1. Ability to print
2. Ability in visual discrimination
3. Knowledge of letter names
4. Awareness that words are composed of letters
5. Awareness that letters stand for sounds
6. Awareness that the writing (spelling) of a word is related to its pronunciation
7. Understanding of *beginning sound*
8. Knowledge of some letter-sound associations

As with any goals, no assumption is being made that all children will reach all of these. They have been listed to remind you of the potential of printing lessons and, secondly, because they affect the type of instruction to be described now. As it is described, you will want to keep the goals in mind.

Initial Lessons

Selecting a letter is the first step. One of the many ways this might be done will be explained with a description of a very effective kindergarten teacher.

She did nothing with writing until November. Earlier, the children had become accustomed to using pencils and paper and had made straight and slanted lines (fences, houses, tepees) and circles (faces, suns, clocks). Meanwhile, the teacher had decided to get writing started by giving attention to *T* and *t*. When it was time, this is how the instruction began.

On the first Tuesday in November, as had become the daily practice, the morning started with comments about the weather, what day it was, and so on. Although a card showing *Tuesday* ordinarily would have been on a bulletin board, it was not there that day in order to give the teacher a reason to say, "I forgot to put up Tuesday," and to print it on the chalkboard as the children watched. Then came the question, "Does anyone know the name of the first letter I made to write Tuesday?" Nobody did, so the teacher answered her own question. She also mentioned it was a capital *T* because *Tuesday* was the name of a day and, like the children's names, began with a capital letter.

She next printed and named a lowercase *t* and asked whether anyone could find a word in the room that started with that. (About a week earlier, a small chart showing *one* and *two* written beneath *1* and *2* had been displayed and discussed.) Several children immediately pointed to the number chart; then the teacher printed *two*. Next she mentioned the possibility of everyone's learning to make *T* and *t*. The children were enthusiastic, thus it was time for the first writing lesson.

It started with the teacher's suggestion to try some "skywriting." (This led to comments about airplanes that write messages in the sky.) The children stood and held up their writing hands; the teacher faced them and demonstrated the correct way to make *T*. Then, as she made it again, the children followed along making their own *T*'s in the air. While they did this, the teacher watched to make sure the direction of their strokes was correct.

Following the air writing, the children sat down and each received a pencil and a piece of unlined paper. After some reminders about how to hold the pencil and where to place the paper, they proceeded to make *T*'s wherever they chose but only on one side of the paper. The teacher circulated among them, correcting strokes that were being made in the wrong sequence or the wrong direction. Subsequently, the same general procedure was followed for lowercase *t,* made on the second side of the paper.

The next day, the kindergartners were treated to a visit in a first-grade room where, as had been planned, the children were having a printing lesson and using lined manuscript paper. The visit created enough interest in writing for the kindergarten teacher to suggest, after they had returned to their own room, that she get some of the special paper used by the first graders. On the following morning it was available, and "big kid" writing lessons began, the first dealing only with capital *T*.

As before, words beginning with *T* were mentioned and written on the chalkboard:

As before, instruction began with skywriting, after which pencils and half sheets of manuscript paper (Figure 6–2) were distributed:

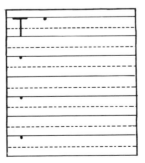

Figure 6–2.

One *T* had been printed on each sheet so that the children would have a close-at-hand model to follow. (Copying from something as far away as a chalkboard can be difficult for young children.) Dots were added to show where to make the first *T* and, further, where each new row of *T*'s was to begin. (The half sheets of paper were used because experiences with other kindergartners had shown that a whole sheet was discouraging for some because it took too many letters to fill it up.) Finally, a model of a completed paper, which had been prepared in advance, was hung up for all to see. (See Figure 6–3.) This had been prepared because past experiences had taught the teacher that a completed model, like a picture, is better than a thousand words for explaining a task.

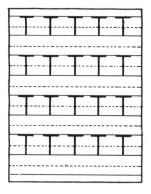

Figure 6–3.

As soon as pencils and paper were ready, the children began their first attempt to use lined paper. By providing the dot, the teacher made sure everyone started his first *T* at the right place. She also offered reminders for making each of the other *T*'s in the first row. When that was completed, the children started the second row; once more, the dot showed the children where to begin. And so the lesson proceeded.

The next writing lesson came several days later, after the children had been talking about Thanksgiving and turkeys. The word *turkey* was used to initiate work on lowercase *t* and to remind the children that once they knew how to make other letters they would be able to write their own words. To show words that started with *T* and *t,* the teacher listed:

Prior to rereading the four words, she casually mentioned that they started not only with the same letter but also with the same sound. (Knowing she would be calling the children's attention to the beginning sound, she did not include words like *Thursday* and *Thanksgiving* in the *T* list.)

The lesson with lowercase *t* was similar to the one for capital *T*. It began with air writing; a finished paper was displayed; and one *t* plus the helpful dots were on the children's sheets. And so another writing lesson was under way.

IMPORTANT FEATURES
OF PRINTING INSTRUCTION

While not all teachers choose to initiate printing instruction in the same way, the illustration in the preceding section exemplifies some practices that are pertinent for any instruction that aims toward the goals listed earlier. For that reason, let me specify those practices now.

1. A special effort should be made to ensure that early experiences with writing are pleasurable, successful, and purposeful. In the illustrative lesson, the teacher had the children visit first-graders and then gave them the "privilege" of using the paper the older children used. To help make first efforts successful, the teacher chose *T* because it is easy to make. Although its lowercase and capital forms were introduced together, writing on the manuscript paper dealt with one at a time, again to ensure success. To provide a purpose for writing, the teacher explained to the children that the ability to make letters would soon allow them to write their own words.

2. Young children need a certain amount of physical activity. Skywriting was used both to get them out of their chairs and to allow the teacher to look for, and correct, erroneous strokes. Because it was compared to the writing done by airplanes, the skywriting added to the children's enjoyment of the lesson.

3. Distractions should be avoided. As was mentioned in an earlier chapter, young children commonly view materials as something to play with. That is why the teacher in the illustration did not distribute pencils and paper until it was time to use them.

4. Correct terminology should be used. The age of the children in the illustration did not keep the teacher from using the terms *capital letter* and *lowercase letter*. She also made sure the name of the letter being taught was mentioned many times.

5. When writing is demonstrated to children, it should be done with special care. That is why the *T*'s on the completed page, plus the sample that was printed

on the children's papers, were perfectly formed. When the teacher was skywriting and facing the children, she was careful to make her strokes in a way that displayed them correctly.

6. Precautions should be taken to minimize a beginner's problems. In the illustration, a page of letters was prepared to clarify the job at hand and was then hung up to serve as a continuous reminder of that job. In addition, half sheets of paper were used to prevent the discouragement that can develop when a task is viewed as being too extensive. Because deciding where to start a letter and a new row can be a problem for beginners, dots were printed on the children's papers to provide guidelines.

7. When printing instruction is viewed as a means for easing children into phonics, certain steps should be included. In the illustration, words that began with *t* were highlighted because the teacher wanted to mention the similarity in the beginning sound of each. (Generally, the initial sound in a word is the easiest to hear as a distinct sound; therefore, it makes sense to start with that.) Although the attention given sounds was very casual during the early lessons, it would gradually become more concentrated as time passed.

8. As time passes, writing lessons can be used to help children arrive at an understanding of such basic instructional language as *same, different, first letter,* and *beginning of a word.*

SUBSEQUENT INSTRUCTION

Even with later lessons, starting with a demonstration of how a letter is formed continues to be a worthwhile practice. Some teachers use transparencies and overhead projections for this, whereas others continue to use skywriting, at least some of the time. In one class in which it was used frequently, the teacher added little touches intermittently to maintain interest. On some days she would print a very large form of the letter on the board; then she and the children pretended to trace it in the air. At other times, she might have her assistant play "A Tisket, A Tasket" on the piano while she and the children made *T* and then *t*. (The same song was used with letters like *C, I, J,* and *L*). *A, B,* and *F* were sometimes written to the tune of "Three Blind Mice," and "Twinkle, Twinkle, Little Star" helped with *b, h,* and *d*. The children's reaction? They loved it. Meanwhile, their teacher was having ample opportunities to make sure that letters were being formed correctly in the air before the children started to cope with the more demanding lines of the manuscript paper.

As lessons progress and children achieve greater facility in making letters, more time can go to preparing for phonics. Since some of the preparation has to do with auditory discrimination, let me comment about that before showing how printing lessons can be beginning phonics lessons. The comments are especially directed to teachers who do not choose to link printing and phonics, and to other teachers who have children who are ready for phonics but not for printing.

Auditory Discrimination Ability

Although a sizeable number of children enter pre–first grade classrooms already able to see differences in the shapes of letters, far fewer have the kind of auditory discrimination ability that is necessary if phonics instruction is to make sense to them (13). What is essential for phonics is the ability to hear that certain speech sounds are alike and that others are different. This immediately suggests an important guideline for anyone trying to teach auditory discrimination: words should be used, *not* musical or environmental sounds.

Distinguishing among speech sounds and hearing that they are similar or dissimilar is not easy for young children. Although astoundingly good language users themselves, they do not use it (nor do any of us) in a way that calls attention to individual sounds. With them, for example, "ball" is *a* sound not a blend of three sounds. More importantly, it is something to throw or catch or own. All this suggests more guidelines for teachers: go slowly with auditory discrimination work, allow for lots of repetition and practice, and make the latter at least somewhat interesting through the use of such things as games. Other kinds of interesting instruction and practice will be described shortly.

For early work with auditory discrimination, short words should be chosen and their initial sounds featured. Later, when children have acquired an understanding of instructional terms like *beginning sound, same sound,* and *different sound* and, in addition, have demonstrated the ability to perceive similar and dissimilar sounds at the beginning of words, they are ready to learn about final sounds. Even though commercially prepared materials always feature rhyming words (e.g., man, can, fan) to help with the concept *same last sound,* my own teaching experiences with young children indicate that they confuse rather than enlighten. Let me explain.

Not knowing any better, I followed manual directions and used workbook pages filled with pictures whose names rhymed. However, it didn't take long to notice that using these pages encouraged the children to equate "words with the same last sound" and "words that rhyme." To illustrate, if I asked a question like, "Do 'bat' and 'sat' end with the same sound?" the children responded, "Yes." If the question was, "Do 'bat' and 'get' end with the same sound?" the same children's response was, "No." While the experience of one person is hardly sufficient to establish facts, I would still suggest that those who work with beginners in phonics at least consider the possibility of bypassing rhyming words in the context of final sounds. If they must be used, save them for work with initial sound substitutions.

To sum up, certain guidelines are being proposed for early work with phonics whether it is separate from, or a part of, printing instruction:

SOME GUIDELINES FOR BEGINNING
INSTRUCTION IN PHONICS

1. Work in auditory discrimination should make use of words, not musical or environmental sounds.
2. Perceiving similarities and differences in speech sounds is difficult for most children. This indicates the need both for slow-paced instruction and for ample practice.
3. Initial sounds in words should be featured first. Later, attention can shift to final sounds.
4. The use of words that rhyme might encourage children to erroneously equate "words that end with the same last sound" and "words that rhyme." To avoid that possibility, rhyming words should be reserved for practice in substituting initial consonant sounds.

Printing Instruction and Beginning Phonics

The point was made earlier that as children acquire facility in making letters, printing instruction can do more with phonics. To be specific, after calling the children's attention to the fact that all the *f* words in a given list start with the same sound (all are read to emphasize this feature), a teacher might ask, "Can *you* think of words that begin with the sound that you hear at the beginning of *fast, food, fish,* and *fun?*" In some cases, they might not yet be ready to respond; that is, they still do not have sufficient ability in auditory discrimination or, perhaps, do not understand the meaning of "begin with the same sound." In other cases, however, teachers are in for a pleasant surprise. I recall one nursery school group in which the teacher had been providing printing instruction much like that being described here. In the spring, I encouraged her to see whether the children could give examples of words beginning with a certain sound; but, even then, she was hesitant, doubting that they could. Nonetheless, she gave it a try and soon found herself facing children who just about fell off their chairs in their eagerness to name words, in this case words beginning with the sound that *b* records. The first contribution? *Bourbon.*

While observing other groups of young children, I have seen the same type of auditory ability displayed. Samples of their contributions follow, along with comments about some of the things that were done when the designated letter received attention during a printing lesson.

M

As was her practice, the teacher printed and named *M* and *m,* then printed and read some words starting with them. An added attraction was a tray of objects (mask, mitten, magnet, map, picture of a man, table mat) covered with a cloth. The teacher said she was a magician—*magician* was dramatically added to the list of words on the chalkboard—and that she was about to make some things appear whose names started with the letter *m*. The objects were uncovered, and the children named them with much enthusiasm. As each was identified, its name was added to the now extensive list. An especially interesting comment from a boy pertained to the table mat, which showed a picture of Donald Duck. He objected, saying, "For *M*, it should be Mickey Mouse."

Following the board work and the effective use of the magic tray, the kindergartners were able to contribute *medicine, milk, monster,* and *magic.*

L

When *L* and *l* were introduced in another classroom, words named by the children were numerous and quick to come. They included *laugh, lamp, look, lap, lawn, ladder, lemon, lantern, leaf, letter, lettuce,* and *Lee.* The children (like others seen in different classrooms) took special delight in the fact that the teacher was running out of space on the chalkboard because they could name so many words that began with the same sound as her original examples: *love, lollipop, Larry,* and *Lincoln.*

Later, art time provided a special surprise, the chance to make paper lollipops. For this, small circles were first cut out of construction paper. Since these were to be the lollipops, the teacher explained, *L* was to be printed on one side and *l* on the other because it was the first letter in *lollipop.* (That point was made explicit to ensure that the children understood the connection between the letter *L* and what they were so eagerly making. Without the direct explanation, some might never see it.) Afterward, each child received a straw through which a piece of pipe cleaner has been pushed to make it firm. (Notice that the teacher did not distribute "sticks" until it was time to use them. Had they been handed out earlier, some children would have played with them when they were supposed to be printing *L* and *l*.) Quickly, the teacher stapled each child's stick to his lollipop; the result was a group of very happy children.

It must be noted that one among them had strenuously objected to calling his a *lollipop.* He insisted it was a *sucker.* The teacher accepted this as a correct name, then wrote *lollipop* and *sucker* on the board. She identified each and asked, "Does anyone know why we're using *lollipop* today even though some of you do call what we made a *sucker?*" Immediately, one child rementioned the connection between *lollipop* and *l.* The teacher continued, "Can anyone think of a reason why I didn't ask you to write the whole word *lollipop* on the circles?" Two responses came quickly. One child said she didn't know how to make all the letters. Another said it was "too fat" to fit. And so an interesting printing-phonics-art lesson came to an end.

H

To provide some variation when *H* and *h* were being introduced, another teacher drew the outline of a large house on the board and asked the children what it was. They answered promptly, so the teacher carefully printed *house* next to the outline and identified *h*. She then inquired, "What else could we call this house? The word I'm thinking of also begins with *h*." Nobody responded. The teacher continued, "Let's play detective. I'll give you a clue. When you leave school you don't say, 'I'm going house.' You say, 'I'm going _____.'" And, of course, everyone called out "home," so that was printed under *house* while the letter *h* was named again.

Following this, the teacher suggested it might be a good idea to write other *h* words inside rather than outside the house in order to keep them warm. (It was January.) Everyone agreed. Eventually, the following were contributed by the children and printed within the outline: *hammer, hat, Halloween* (this word gave the teacher the chance to identify capital *H* and to explain why *Halloween* started with a capital letter), *hunt, harness, hot* ("hot dog" was the suggestion, so the teacher explained why only *hot* could be printed), *hand, head,* and *heart*. To stress the similarity of their beginning sound, the teacher concluded the phonics part of the lesson by reading all the words named. Then printing instruction began with air writing.

P

On the day I was visiting in one kindergarten, *P* and *p* had been selected for a printing-phonics lesson. In order to write the *forty-one* words suggested by the children, the teacher—with much fanfare—covered three chalkboards. Rather than take the space to list all forty-one, let me just say that the examples included such words as "Peyton Place" (at the time of the visit it was a television program) and such long responses as, "Peter, Peter, pumpkin eater."

T

What one teacher did with *T* and *t* was described earlier. Here, let me mention what another chose to do. In this case, much more was done with the sound that it records, because the lesson came later in the school year. This meant that the children could learn to print *T* and *t* more rapidly and would be more adept at hearing initial sounds.

As was her custom, the teacher began by writing a capital *T*. She identified it and immediately heard from Tommy that it was the first letter in his name. Consequently, under *T* went *Tommy*.

She then said that she knew another name starting with *T*. She explained that it was not a child's name but, instead, the name of a tuba. This prompted questions about a tuba, all of which were answered with the help of a picture of one. Next, the children tried to guess its proper name but were unsuccessful. Consequently, the teacher told them as she printed it. The board now showed:

This lesson also had a special surprise, a recording of the song "Tubby the Tuba." After it was played and obviously enjoyed, the teacher asked for other words that started like *Tommy, Tubby,* and *tuba.* The following were offered by the children and printed by the teacher: *television, telephone, table, turkey, tea, teeth, tongue, train, tiny, trick, tent, tonsils, towel,* and *truck.* To summarize the phonics part of the lesson, the teacher read all the words, commenting again about the similarity of their beginning sound. Then printing instruction began.

To illustrate still other words I have heard young children offer during printing lessons, let me list some in the order in which they were mentioned. It happens that all were suggested by kindergartners.

F

flower, flea, Flipper, floor, feather, fan, Friday, first, French, fur, fish, fork, flag, four, father, fence

W

wagon, wasp, wine, worm, waiting, water, watermelon, wife, wiggle

N

newspaper, nickel, napkin, nursery, numeral, nurse, needle, nail, nun, nest, Nixon, nothing, name, nap, no, neighbor

V

violet, vegetable, Venus, vacation, vase, Valentine, vacuum, valley, volcano

U

umbrella, umpire, under, ugly, uncle, usher, us, up

C

cute, coffee, coffee cake, coke, comb, carrot, cookie, candle, cap, coat

PRACTICE FOR PRINTING

Even consistently superior instruction does not eliminate the need for practice. The purpose of this section, therefore, is to outline characteristics of printing practice that is both productive and suitable for younger children.

The best kind begins in the mind of the teacher who views it not as repetition of the same thing done in the same way but as repetition done in different ways—with different trimmings, if you will. This means that it is important to look for ways to vary the repetition that is necessary for the development of a motor skill like printing. With young children, this is not difficult. Just changing from black pencils to red ones—or adding some music—is enough to give them the feeling of doing something different. I have also seen other small but successful variations, such as making letters on a lined chalkboard or in sand in a paper plate. In one classroom, practice at the board was sometimes carried on with large brushes that had been dipped in water. This was known as "magic practice" because as the water dried, the letters disappeared. Whether done with chalk or a brush, chalkboard practice is highly desirable because, unlike skywriting, it gives children a chance to see what they have written.

Another feature of practice that is both productive and tolerable is an amount of repetition that is neither tiresome nor more than what is needed. Here I cannot help but recall two kindergartners, both boys but in different schools, who were willing to practice a letter only until they knew—and knew they knew —how to make it well. If the letter happened to be an easy one (*I* and *i,* for instance), they would write it just a few times and no more. On the other hand, if the selected letter was difficult, one could expect to find them trying to squeeze into every line of letters more samples than were required. While no generalization can be drawn from just two children, the behavior of these boys is a reminder to avoid unnecessary practice.

And that reminder suggests the next characteristic from the teacher's point of view: select only those letters that need to be improved. This means that when printing lessons get under way, they should be interspersed with practice sessions focusing on what turned out to be difficult-to-make letters. With certain ones, just about all the children will need the extra practice; with others, only a few will require it. During practice periods, therefore, different children will often be working on different letters. It also is likely that some will be doing something else.

PRINTING WORDS

Since the reason for printing instruction is to enable children to write words, attention should go to them as soon as possible.

One teacher initiated the attention by taking advantage of the children's perpetual self-interest. Thus, she started with *me*. First she printed it on the board; some children knew what it said and spontaneously identified it. Then, at the request of the teacher, the children named the two letters. (Each had been identified and practiced in an earlier printing lesson.) Next the teacher suggested that it might be a good idea to practice printing *me* because self-portraits (one of the Christmas presents for parents) were to be made at art time, and *me* would be a good label.

After practicing *m* and *e* in the air, each child received paper (Figure 6–4).

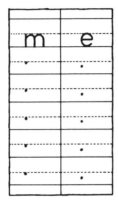

Figure 6–4.

To specify the task and to serve as a reminder of it, a finished model was displayed in the front of the room. (See Figure 6–5.)

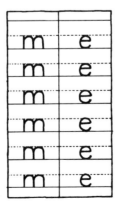

Figure 6–5.

The directions were to print *me* five times. When art began, the children could select their best *m* and *e,* cut them out, and paste the two rectangular pieces close together (to emphasize the wholeness of the word) at the bottom of the self-made portraits. Motivation and enthusiasm were high; in addition, each letter had been introduced and practiced earlier. The result was a first attempt at writing a word that brought both enjoyment and success.

What is always a source of enjoyment for young children is the ability to print their own names. (See Figure 6–6.) Even teachers who bypass other printing instruction would be wise to allow time for practice with names if for no other reason than the enjoyment children experience.

Instruction in printing first names can begin with attention to initial letters. One teacher started with the first letter plus a period, explaining to the children that the period would take the place of the remaining letters until they learned to make them. What she was doing, of course, was paving the way to an understanding of *abbreviation.*

Figure 6–6. Eight Samples of Name Writing at Mid-Year in Kindergarten

Practice with initial letters in names can be carried on much like the writing practice already described. Now, though, a teacher will be printing different letters on different papers, all of which serve as close-at-hand models as the children attempt their own versions. To replace air writing, impossible because of the variety of letters, the teacher will move from child to child, offering suggestions and, whenever necessary, changing erroneous formations.

Soon the children can practice the first two letters and, before long, all of them. As the various letters are being added, the children can also get some practice in noting their sequence. For this, a small name card can be given to each one, plus an envelope containing all the letters in the name. A more permanent name card might also be attached to each child's desk. Covered with contact paper, its letters can be traced.

As time passes and children routinely sign their names to many things, they often get careless in forming letters. That is why it is a good idea to schedule time periodically for attention to more careful efforts. For this, the name cards can serve as models, even though they might not have been used for some time. Very helpful, too, are samples of the children's earlier attempts at name writing, which were done with greater care.

COMPOSING

For both teacher and children, printing instruction and practice should always be seen as a means to an end: ability to write words and, with them, to express thoughts. (Lucy has the right idea in Figure 6–7.) Such a perspective is important for teachers because it discourages turning printing lessons into isolated, monotonous drill. A correct perspective is important for the children because, by making their work meaningful, it provides motivation.

At first, when both printing and composing skills are limited, children's writing efforts might be as brief as one- or two-word captions for pictures they have drawn. Figure 6–8 shows the efforts of two kindergartners. The first child

© 1978 United Feature Syndicate, Inc.

Figure 6-7.

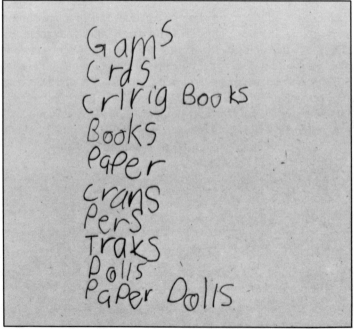

Figure 6–8. Samples of Beginning Efforts in Composing

captioned her picture of a sea serpent. The second listed the plans she made for the trip her family was going to take when school ended. Such independent writing efforts are most apt to occur in classrooms where, earlier, the teacher took the time to print what children dictated. Such dictation was illustrated in Chapter 4 (Figure 4–2) when language experience materials were being discussed as one way to help young children see the connection between spoken and written language.

Until a little independence in printing and spelling is acquired, material that is more extensive than one or two words (e.g., descriptions, invitations, thank-you notes, messages for greeting cards) can continue to be dictated by the children and printed by the teacher. For instance, after discussing with the children how they feel when they are alone, a teacher could write something like that shown below. Such an account serves as a summary of the discussion, as a model of the way thoughts can be written, and as a reminder for the children of why they are learning to print.

> When We're Alone
> When we're alone it's not so nice.
> We feel scared sometimes.
> We want somebody to come home.
> Then we won't be alone anymore.

Children's composing efforts can get started with parts of sentences. In this case—again to serve as a model—a teacher could print the beginning of a sentence on the board, then let children suggest endings. For example:

> If I were as tall as a giraffe
> I wouldn't need to stand on a chair.
> I would be bigger than my big brother.
> I'd have to get new clothes.

Other beginnings for sentences can be on paper. Children could choose one, then write an ending themselves. Suitable material might be something like these:

> If I had a dollar
>
> If I were as small as a mouse

Later, other beginnings might lead to more extensive conclusions. For instance:

I wish	I never	I can't
I always	I can	I like

Since the reason for these early composing efforts is to encourage children to express their thoughts and feelings and observations, requirements such as correct spellings can be laid aside temporarily. (Misspellings, incidentally, offer useful information about what needs to be stressed in phonics instruction.) However, since all this early writing is for communication, children do need to be helped to see the significance of leaving ample space between words. (The width of their index finger can be used as a guideline for where to start a word that follows another in a sentence. A few demonstrations by a teacher are enough to explain the procedure.)

Once children are doing more extensive composing, it is helpful to establish a special place as a writing center. Separated from the rest of the classroom by a mobile bulletin board or by a table or bookshelves, the center should allow for self-selected and uninterrupted opportunities to write. With this as the goal, centers ought to have pencils, pens, and crayons; various sizes of lined and unlined paper; models of the alphabet; and picture dictionaries to help with spelling. If it is to be an inviting place, other materials should be available, too. Interesting pictures, for instance, often prompt equally interesting writing. At a more elementary level, papers with titles or unfinished sentences can serve as starters.

For children who might choose the center as a place to improve their printing, copies of a few writing workbooks could be available along with alphabet models. Occasionally, covers of large boxes can be filled with sand to provide for a special kind of practice. Small, portable chalkboards will be attractive, too. A few short papers, carefully printed by a teacher, might be displayed, eventually to be replaced by the children's own work. (Samples of children's work are shown in Figures 6–9 and 6–10.) Since children doing this kind of composing are providing others with something to read, this is the time to underscore requirements such as carefully printed letters and ample space between words.

A BRIEF OVERVIEW: CHAPTERS FOUR, FIVE, AND SIX

Although chapters 4, 5, and 6 discussed different aspects of a language arts program, the topics they covered are closely connected. All three, for instance, were written with reading in mind. Underlying all three, too, is recognition of the fundamental importance of oral language. Thus it is not an accident that Chapter 5, which deals specifically with that topic, is the longest of the three.

Any nursery school or kindergarten teacher who, for whatever reason, is opposed to starting reading instruction before first grade would do well to read Chapter 5 especially carefully. This recommendation reflects the belief that even though pre–first grade programs have no universal obligation to teach reading, every single one of them bears a serious responsibility to add to children's competency in oral language. Since success with reading is so dependent upon that competency, Chapter 5 also merits careful reading by teachers who are busy teaching reading.

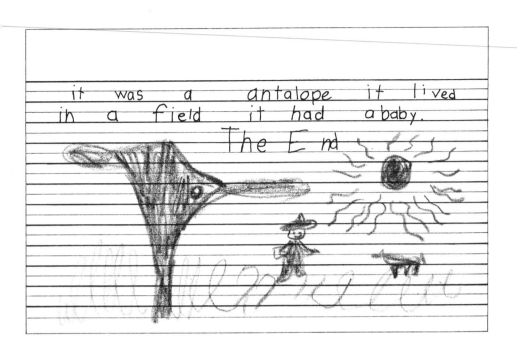

it was a antalope it lived
in a field it had a baby.
The End

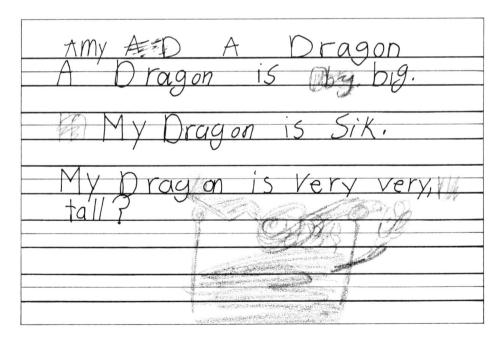

Amy A̶E̶D A Dragon
A Dragon is aby big.
My Dragon is Sik.
My Dragon is very very,
tall?

Figure 6–9. Children's Early Composing Efforts

> What is a friend?
>
> A friend is some one who is fun.
> My friend are Connie
> Paula Julie Kataleen
> Jana Angela
> Rebecca

> I saw a red spiter and
> it had perpple spots he looked
> sille. and it had babys all
> difrot colrs and thay looked
> sille too. Kathleen

Figure 6–10. Samples of Slightly More Advanced Writing

Even though Chapters 4, 5, and 6 each looked at instructional programs from a different perspective, all three underscored the importance of teaching in ways that will be attractive to children. Interesting procedures and activities were highlighted not on the assumption that teachers should be entertainers but in recognition of the fact that attention and achievement go hand in hand.

Since these chapters did deal with different pieces of the same instructional program, it would be helpful now to reread the three in succession in order to see how the pieces fit together.

REVIEW

1. Chapter 6 was directed to teachers of young children, yet some of the points stated or implied in it about the requirements of effective instruction apply to any level—nursery school through college. Skim through Chapter 6 to identify those generally applicable requirements.

2. One characteristic of effective instructors is the ability to do educationally significant things in interesting ways. A kindergarten teacher I know is excellent in this regard. For example, when she provides practice in visual discrimination, she might do such things as show Alpha Bits (pieces of cereal) on an overhead projector, or have the children group blocks according to the letters they display. What are some other ways to make visual discrimination practice interesting for young children?

3. Almost inevitably, pictures enter into practice with auditory discrimination. For instance, teachers commonly have children name pictured objects and tell which of the names begin with the same sound. When pictures do figure in such practice, should they be labeled? That is, should a picture of a ball be labeled *ball*? Reason out the answer, keeping in mind that the nature of a goal indicates what is desirable.

4. Let's say that you are teaching children to print *S* and *s* in a way that follows the recommendations of Chapter 6. Thus, you have the following words on the board:

snow	Sue
six	Saturday
seven	September
salt	

Having read the seven words to the children to highlight the similarity of their beginning sound, you ask them, "Can you think of any other word that starts with the sound that you hear at the beginning of all these words?" One child responds, "Cynthia." How should *you* respond?

REFERENCES

1. Blatt, Gloria T. "Playing with Language." *Reading Teacher* XXXI (February, 1978), 487–491.
2. Carnegie, Dale. *How to Win Friends and Influence People.* New York: Simon and Schuster, 1936.
3. Chomsky, Carol. "Write First, Read Later." *Childhood Education* XLVII (March, 1971), 296–299.
4. Cutts, Warren. "Does the Teacher Really Matter?" *Reading Teacher* XXVIII (February, 1975), 449–452.
5. Dewey, John. "The Primary-Education Fetich." *The Forum* XXV (May, 1898), 315–328.
6. Durkin, Dolores. *Children Who Read Early.* New York: Teachers College Press, Columbia University, 1966.
7. Durkin, Dolores. "A Language Arts Program for Pre–First Grade Children: Two-Year Achievement Report." *Reading Research Quarterly* V (Summer, 1970), 534–565.
8. Durrell, Donald D. "First-Grade Reading Success Study: A Summary." *Journal of Education* CXL (February, 1958), 2–6.
9. Enstrom, E. A. "But How Soon Can We *Really* Write?" *Elementary English* XLV (March, 1968), 360–363.
10. Flesch, Rudolph. *Why Johnny Can't Read and What You Can Do About It.* New York: Harper and Brothers, 1955.
11. Freeman, Frank N. "An Evaluation of Manuscript Writing." *Elementary School Journal* XXXVI (February, 1936), 446–455.
12. Hall, Mary Ann; Moretz, Sara A.; and Statom, Jodellano. "Writing before Grade One—A Study of Early Writers." *Language Arts* LIII (May, 1976), 582–585.
13. Paradis, Edward, and Peterson, Joseph. "Readiness Training Implications from Research." *Reading Teacher* XXVIII (February, 1975), 445–448.
14. Patrick, G. T. W. "Should Children under Ten Learn to Read and Write?" *Popular Science Monthly* LIV (February, 1899), 382–392.
15. Read, Charles. "Pre-school Children's Knowledge of English Phonology." *Harvard Educational Review* XLI (February, 1971), 1–34.
16. Richek, Margaret Ann. "Readiness Skills That Predict Initial Word Learning Using Two Different Methods of Instruction." *Reading Research Quarterly* XIII, no. 2 (1977–1978), 200–222.
17. Robinson, Helen M. "News and Comment: Methods of Teaching Beginning Readers." *Elementary School Journal* LIX (May, 1959), 419–426.
18. Samuels, S. Jay. "The Effect of Letter-Name Knowledge on Learning to Read." *American Educational Research Journal* IX (Winter, 1972), 65–74.

III

Early Instructional Materials

Unquestionably, the ability to make judicious decisions is one of the hallmarks of a truly professional person. For the teaching profession, the ability to make such decisions about what to teach and to whom to teach it would naturally rank high on any list of priorities. This prompts the question, Is the content of instruction always determined by teachers? Stated differently, Is every teacher a professional teacher?

If "determine what will be taught" is an essential requirement, then research indicates that not all teachers are. For example, one survey carried out by EPIE (Educational Products Information Exchange Institute) reached the conclusion that 95 percent of what is done in classrooms can be attributed to commercially prepared materials (2). In another study, in which thirty-nine classrooms were visited, teachers were found spending much more time on giving and checking assignments than on instructing (1). Almost without exception, the assignments originated in workbooks and ditto sheets. In still another study, reported by Goodlad and Klein in *Behind the Classroom Door,* a similar conclusion was reached: "Textbooks and workbooks dominate the teaching-learning process" (3, p. 81).

If all the materials that are being referred to were selected in relation to what children needed and were ready to learn, concern would not be warranted. The fact is, however, that what comes next in a book often determines how teachers and children spend their time. Goodlad and Klein describe this dependence by saying, "We are forced to conclude that the vast majority of teachers in our sample [158 classrooms in 67 schools in 26 school districts] was oriented more to a drive for coverage of certain materials than to a reasonably clear perception of behavior sought in their pupils" (3, p. 78).

Although nursery schools and kindergartens did not figure in any of the studies just mentioned, the more widespread that reading instruction becomes at those levels, the more will commercial materials roll off the presses. The prospect of that occurring, coupled with the basic importance of materials in any instructional program, suggests the need for a chapter that singles out materials for special attention. That is what Chapter 7 does.

CHAPTER

7

Language Experience and Other Homemade Materials

PREVIEW

As used in this book, *instructional material* refers to anything that displays words. Within that framework, instructional materials include: textbooks, library books, newspapers, maps, magazines, greeting cards, letters, brochures, pamphlets, catalogues, telephone directories, schedules, calendars, television commercials, timetables, license plates, pencils, recipes, comics, menus, coupons, road signs, neon signs, and labeled boxes, packages, and cans.

Although it is homemade materials that get attention in Chapter 7, what is prepared commercially should not be thought of as something that must be shunned at all costs by those who work with young children. Many times I have seen these materials being used in ways that not only promoted individualized instruction but also added to the children's enjoyment of school. Used occasionally for a pedagogically sound reason, even something like a workbook page or ditto sheet requires neither an apology nor an excuse.

What must *always* be shunned, however, is a situation that is all too common in elementary schools:

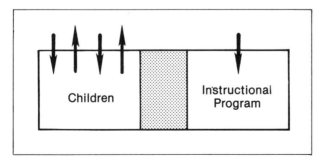

Portrayed above is the school in which the instructional program is "set" at each grade level (usually by commercial materials) in spite of the fact that, each year, the children change. It is as if a wall kept the children from having an effect on the program.

Teachers who want to make sure that children *do* affect programs use language experience materials. Begun in Chapter 4, the discussion of these important materials is continued in Chapter 7.

In addition to discussing and illustrating the use of language experience materials for instructional purposes, Chapter 7 describes other homemade materials that allow for interesting practice. The chapter closes by calling attention to additional bulletin-board displays, each designed to help reach a preestablished goal.

As mentioned on page 187, one distinctive characteristic of superior teachers is their ability to make informed decisions about instructional goals. Once they decide what needs to be taught, they proceed to consider the materials that can help attain them. Ideally, the selected materials not only will be instrumental in achieving instructional goals but also will be of interest to the children. Clearly, the twofold contribution points in the direction of language experience materials.

LANGUAGE EXPERIENCE MATERIALS

Based on function, language experience materials divide into *contactual, instructional,* and *practice* materials (4). Reasons for the first type are to bring young children into contact with written language in meaningful, personal ways; to point up the connection between spoken and written language; to teach the meaning of *word*; to show how empty space functions in establishing word boundaries; and to display the left-to-right, top-to-bottom orientation of written English. As a result of early contacts with language experience materials, some children begin to read; but getting reading ability started is not the central concern.

The contactual function of language experience materials was dealt with in Chapter 4, starting on page 100. Rereading those pages will allow for a review of the earliest uses.

Later uses, which are the concern now, aim directly toward the start and continuation of reading ability. Within that framework, language experience materials can help develop (and review) reading vocabularies, explain and illustrate capitalization and punctuation, and provide words for teaching about (and reviewing) letter-sound relationships and word structure.

Omitted from the list of contributions, as you may have noticed, is help with word meanings and comprehension. That was not mentioned because when material pertains to a particular group of children and their experiences, the meaning of individual words or connected text presents no problem. This allows for concentrated attention to other aspects of reading ability.

Instructional Goals and Language Experience Materials

As with any other kind of material, how language experience materials ought to be used depends on *why* they are being used. The dependent relationship can be shown with a couple of examples.

Developing Reading Vocabularies.   While there is neither the time nor the need to teach every new word with language experience materials, teaching some with its help makes learning to read more personal and interesting. Let me illustrate this (along with showing how goals affect procedures) by describing what one teacher did after gathering some kindergartners together near a chalkboard in order to teach *red*.

Teacher:	This really is a beautiful morning, isn't it? It was a good morning to look at things on the way to school. As I was driving, I saw leaves that were the most beautiful colors— green, yellow, red, orange. Did *you* notice anything as you walked to school?
Tonia:	My mother drove me.
Annamarie:	I saw some noisy motorcycles!
Teacher:	What color were they?
Annamarie:	I don't know. They were too noisy.
Teacher:	David, what did you see?
David:	I saw Tommy's new bike.
Teacher:	What color is it?
David:	I forget.
Teacher:	Let's see if we can think of some things whose colors we can remember. When you do think of something, I'll write what you say up here [points to the chalkboard]. I'll pick one color to get started. I'll take red. That's a good, bright color for a good, bright morning. Let me show you what the word *red* looks like [prints *red* on board]. What does this word say?
Children:	Red.
Teacher:	To help you remember it, let's spell it [points to letters].
Children:	R, e, d.
Teacher:	What does this word say?
Children:	Red.
Teacher:	I'll name one thing that's red. A fire truck is red. Watch me write what I just said. Now I'll read it [points to each word]. "A fire truck is red." What does this word say [points to red]?
Children:	Red.
Teacher:	Let's see if you can read all the words I just wrote [points to each].
Children:	A fire truck is red.
Teacher:	Can you tell me something else that's red? George?
George:	Chicken pox and measles are red.
Teacher:	Wonderful! Watch as I write what George just told us.

Eventually the chalkboard showed:

> A fire truck is red.
> Chicken pox and measles are red.
> Lipstick is red.
> A red crayon is red.
> Part of the flag is red.
> My daddy's pants are red.

What else is done with *red* to ensure that it will be remembered depends on what the children know and on how quickly they learn. If their entire reading vocabulary is *blue* and *green,* the teacher could use a ditto sheet showing an outline of something like a clown whose clothes can be colored according to one-word directions: *red, blue, green.* If vocabularies are slightly larger, they may allow for practice with phrases. In this case, the teacher can ask individual children to read aloud some cards like these:

| red, white, and blue | the green toy | a little red hat |

To personalize activities with *red,* the next step might be an opportunity for the children to draw whatever they wish, as long as it has some connection with red. All could start with "Red" printed at the top of their paper. (This might be the time to give attention to titles and capitalization.) Later, as children finish their drawings, the teacher or aide can print whatever comments or descriptions they wish to add to them.

Other Instructional Goals.   To show how other abilities and understandings can be initiated or reviewed, let me list two more examples of language experience materials and, under each, some of the instructional possibilities. (What is actually possible varies because what children are ready for varies.)

The first example resulted from a discussion of spring in a first grade. Children's contributions provided the content; instructional goals determined how the teacher transformed them into sentences.

<u>Look for Spring</u>
Look for the sun in the sky.
Look for bugs in trees.
Look for green grass.
Look for robins.

<u>Instructional Possibilities</u>
Reading vocabulary

   Teach *for.*
   Review *the, in, look.*

Distinction in meaning

four (taught previously)
and *for*

Way to denote plural

bugs, robins

The next example is from another first grade in which one child received special attention each week. Written descriptions of a child were dictated by a small group whose members changed weekly. The descriptions were printed by the teacher (first on the board, then on primary chart paper), read and used by everyone, and featured on a bulletin board entitled "The Kid of the Week."

Guess Who?
This is a girl.
She has very long hair.
Sometimes she wears a ribbon
    in her hair.
She has a new baby sister.
Who is she?

Instructional Possibilities
Vocabulary

Teach *new, sister.*
Review *guess, who, girl,
    has, hair, this, she.*

Punctuation

Review function of question mark.

Steps in Developing Language Experience Materials

No set of rules exists for teachers who choose to use language experience material. What are listed below, therefore, are generally useful guidelines, not inevitable steps that must be followed in a given order.

Selection of goal(s)
Selection of topic
Discussion
Composing material
Follow-up activities

Comments about each step follow.

Selection of Goal(s).   The underlying reason for using language experience material is to make learning to read both personal and relevant. Other more specific goals should be selected prior to choosing a topic to write about. This sequence is necessary because the nature of the goals usually affects both the choice and the development of a topic. To illustrate, if one specific goal is to help children understand that the end of a thought doesn't always come at the end of a line, a teacher has to see to it that some sentences are either longer or shorter than a line. On the other hand, if a goal is to teach some of the vocabulary that is required for reading certain commercially prepared material, then the selected topic needs to be one that allows for use of those words, ideally more than once.

While it is important to have definite goals at the outset, how material develops may allow for attention to other needs. If some or all of the children are struggling to remember *and, the,* and *what,* for example, and these words end up being in the material, it should be used to review them.

Selection of Topic.   Although teachers may have to work at motivating children to read commercially prepared material, that should not be the case with language experience material. If it is, the wrong topic was selected. Visits to classrooms have shown that "right" topics include:

Toys with Wheels	Haircuts	At the Hatchery
Melting Snow	Puddles	Mumps
Halloween Masks	When We Are Older	If We Had Our Way
Buttons	Something in My	What Happened to Our
Icy Sidewalks	Eye	Gerbil?

As all the sample topics point up, looking for exotic things to write about is hardly necessary or desirable, since children are most interested in what is near at hand, in what is happening now, and in what relates to themselves.

While a great deal of language experience material will be narration, other forms result from the need to extend an invitation, to express appreciation, to explain a process, or to summarize. In one recently visited classroom, a bulletin board displayed a very interesting type of summary. To the left was a simple bar graph that summarized the colors of cars seen on a recent walk through the neighborhood and the frequency with which each was seen. To the right was a group-dictated account of additional observations about the same cars. To the right of the account was a long column of photographs of cars taken from dealers' brochures, each labeled with a car's name.

While the board effectively demonstrated various ways of communicating, it also illustrated how the real world can enter into efforts to learn to read. Along with all the other examples of language experience material, it points up how restrictive it is to think of instructional materials only in terms of textbooks, workbooks, and ditto sheets.

Discussion.   Ideally, both the content and the sentences for language experience material originate with the children. Certain instructional goals, however, make teachers more active participants. In either case, involving children in the discussion and development of a topic is important for generating both overall content and specific sentences. Depending on the topic, the children, and the pre-established goals, a discussion may be entirely spontaneous or, on the other hand, structured with questions like: How did you feel when that happened? How many were there? What did you think when you heard that? What color was it? Did you get a chance to touch it? What happened first? Why do you think they did that? At other times, the use of pictures, objects, a film, or a story might be the best way to get children talking. Whatever the stimulus, some discussion is important.

Composing the Material.   Whether a sentence comes from a child, comes from a child but is edited, or comes directly from the teacher, it should be carefully but quickly printed while the children watch. Each word and then the sentence is read first by the teacher and next by the children with as much help as is necessary. Once the entire account has been printed, the children read all of it.

Follow-up Activities.   Only if a topic captures everyone's sustained attention should its development take place with an entire class. Even when a whole class does participate, the material may eventually be used in different ways with different children. In fact, what happens after material is composed varies as much as material, children, and goals vary. If an entire class has been involved, some of its members might be asked to copy and illustrate the material, to write their own ideas on the same topic, or to do unrelated work. This frees a teacher to use the account with others in order to ask questions about punctuation, to have them identify certain words, to compare related words (e.g., *snow* and *snowy*), to call attention to similarity in spelling and sound, and so on.

If, for whatever reason, material has value for more than one day, it should be transferred to chart paper. If each child needs a copy, the account can be typed and duplicated.

PRACTICE MATERIALS

All too often, the need for practice brings to mind workbooks and ditto sheets. Why that is an undesirably narrow perspective is illustrated in the samples of interesting practice listed below. To specify the priority of goal selection for practice as well as for instruction, each sample starts with a statement of a goal viewed from a teacher's perspective.

SAMPLES OF PRACTICE

Goal: To provide practice in identifying selected words in the context of phrases.

Materials: Box painted blue to represent pond; fish-shaped pieces of construction paper on which phrases are printed and to which a paper clip is attached; long, thin stick (such as a florist uses in arranging flowers) with a string tied to one end; a magnet tied to the end of the string.

Procedure: Place the fish in a box. Individuals in a small group take turns fishing for a phrase. If the children read their phrases correctly, they keep the fish; otherwise, the fish go back into the pond.

Goal: To review the sounds recorded by *m* and *t* in initial position.

Materials: Two plastic clothes baskets, one showing a card on which *m* has been printed and the other displaying a card with *t*; two large balls.

Procedure: When inclement weather requires indoor recess, playing "Phonics Basketball" is one way to spend the time. Two teams are selected, and a member of each gets a ball. Members take turns listening to the teacher say a word that begins with *m* or *t*. If a child throws his ball into the correct basket, he moves to the end of the line, eventually getting another turn. Otherwise, he sits down. At some stipulated time, the team with the most members standing is declared the winner. Other children form two more teams, and the game continues.

Goal: To provide practice in identifying numerals from 1 to 5 and in counting from 1 to 5.

Materials: Collections of paper squares, pebbles, buttons, straws, toothpicks, popsicle sticks, etc.; numeral cards.

Procedure: Distribute one of the above collections among a small group of children. Show a numeral and have them count out that number of items.

Goal: To help children learn to read *family,* and to provide printing practice.

Materials: Store catalogues.

Procedure: Following a discussion of families, have children cut out people figures to match the makeup of their families. After the figures are pasted on paper, have the children label their collections *family*.

Goal:	To review the sound recorded by *f*.
Materials:	Paper from which hand fans can be made; small dittoed pictures of objects whose names begin with *f*—for example, face, fence, flower, foot, football, frog, fountain, feather, flag, fire, fan.
Procedure:	Have children make fans with wide folds. Then distribute the pictures, which will be named by all, colored, cut out, and pasted in the folds as a decoration. (Be sure the connection between the fans, the names of the pictures, and the sound recorded by *f* is made explicit. Otherwise, the activity will be no more than a cut-and-paste exercise.)
Goal:	To add baby animal words to children's speaking vocabulary (e.g., *lamb, piglet, calf, colt*).
Materials:	Clay and small rectangular pieces of paper for labels.
Procedure:	After giving attention to animal vocabulary through pictures and stories, have each child make one pair of clay animals— a horse and a colt, for instance. Later, display the pairs on a table, each with a printed label showing the names.
Goal:	To provide practice in identifying letters from *a* to *g*.
Materials:	Piano; cardboard keyboard made the same size as an actual one with each white key labeled *a* to *g;* dittoed copies of: c c g g a a g f f e e d d c.
Procedure:	Have children read aloud the names of the letters on the dittoed sheets. Place the cardboard keyboard, standing up, behind the corresponding keys of the piano. Ask the children to rename the letters so that you will know which keys to play. Play as they read. The results will be part of two familiar songs ("Twinkle, Twinkle, Little Star" and "Alphabet Song") and a group of delighted children.

While it is a real joy for teachers to have children who are delighted with their efforts, superior instructional programs *are* superior not because they entertain but because they teach. Although all the foregoing activities will appeal to children, they are educationally significant only when used with those who have not yet achieved their goals. If the goals have been realized, the activities are just busy work. And while interesting busy work is better than dull busy work, it is still busy work.

The same comments apply to the teacher-made materials shown in Figures 7.1–7.3. With these, the teachers composed, typed, and duplicated material that

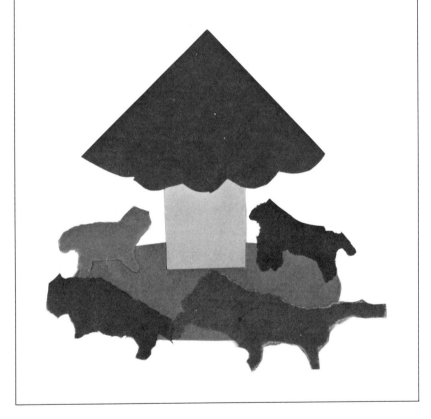

Come With Me

1. I see something.
2. Look boys and girls.
3. I want to ride.
4. See me ride up and down.
5. See me jump.
6. See me jump fast.
7. "Come ride with me," said Diane.
8. See me ride the funny merry-go-round.
9. It is yellow, green, red and blue.

Figure 7-1. Art and Reading

Beginning readers sometimes have problems keeping the place when sentences in a continuous text figure in practice. To help, each sentence can be numbered so that if a child does lose his place, he can be directed back to it with a reference to a numeral.

199

Figure 7–2. Homemade Material for Word Practice

This teacher-composed account has numbered sentences to help chil-dren keep the place. Sometimes paper markers (narrow, rectangular pieces of construction paper) are also used to keep children from getting lost on a page. Should they be? Like all other crutches, a marker should be used only if it seems necessary and, secondly, only for as long as the need exists. If used, a marker should be placed above what is being read, since putting it underneath a line (as is the custom) fosters line rather than sentence reading.

I See Something

1. I see something.
2. "It can jump," said Tom.
3. It can jump up and down.
4. The something can go fast.
5. "It likes to play," said Kane.
6. My something is funny.
7. It is my dog.

Figure 7–3. Comprehending

Practice in visualizing the picture that is conveyed through print can get started early. Above is one child's conception of what is communicated in a simple text. Using the names of children in a class personalizes the activity.

provided for word practice. Two of the three examples also show how reading practice and art activities can be combined in enjoyable and fruitful ways.

BULLETIN BOARD DISPLAYS

Thoughtfully assembled bulletin boards can be equally productive. How they allow for summaries was discussed and illustrated earlier, starting on page 145. Important reminders for all bulletin board displays were also given. Now, Figures 7.4–7.8 show additional boards, each offering practice to which children responded with much enthusiasm. Kindly examine those materials and the commentary about each one now.

A SUMMARY

Whether a bulletin board display or a candy wrapper, instructional material should be viewed as something that assists a teacher in carrying out instructional decisions based on needs. Their correct function can be reinforced with a comparison of two teachers:

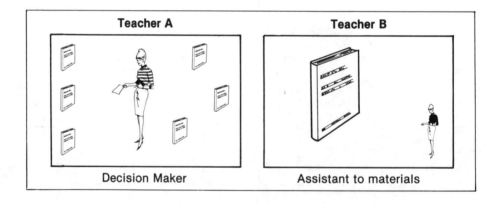

Teacher A is thoroughly knowledgeable about instructional materials and makes decisions about what to use (or make) after other decisions are reached about what needs to be taught, reviewed, or practiced. In contrast, Teacher B allows materials to run her program; she does what they suggest.

(Text is continued on page 208)

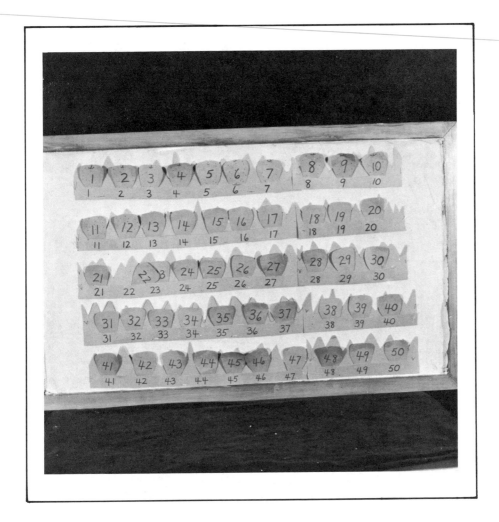

Figure 7–4. Numeral Identification

Strawberries placed in rows help with numerals in a variety of ways. At the start, children can be given numbered strawberries to be put in the correct place on the board. This simply requires matching.

Later, as children learn the names of numerals, a teacher can call one out, after which a child will pick that strawberry.

When children learn to print numerals, the same bulletin-board display will be useful again. Individual children can be directed to pick certain strawberries and to practice making the numerals shown on them. Still later, the display will help children understand the concept ten.

Were the strawberries labeled with letters or words, similar procedures could be followed to achieve other goals.

Figure 7–5. Teaching the Sound Recorded by D

To initiate a discussion of the sound that d *records at the beginning of words, a board displaying the outline of two doors, each with a doorknob, can be prepared. Once children have identified the doors and talked about the meaning of* doorknob, *it is time to write* door *and* doorknob *on a chalkboard and to point out that they begin with* d. *Next, the children can be asked to listen for their beginning sound. (The teacher reads the words aloud.) Following this, the children can identify the objects attached to the board and, in this way, hear still more words that begin with* d. *As the teacher writes the words, the children also have the chance to see them. To summarize, the teacher will read the total list.*

Figure 7–6. Practice with Words, Phrases, and Sentences

After children are acquainted with Humpty Dumpty, a display can be prepared for practice with word identification. (Some of the bricks in the wall have flaps that can be picked up to show words, phrases, and brief sentences.) The display is used by having children take turns being Humpty, which they do by holding a miniature figure resembling him. With Humpty in hand, a child tries to climb the wall by reading the words and sentences. An incorrect response means that, like Humpty, he takes "a great fall." Another child is then given the chance to climb. If he is successful, his name is printed on a miniature figure.

Figure 7–7. Practice with Word Identification

This display is an adaptation of the fishing pond that was described when samples of practice were given earlier. For the board, a pond was made by covering the lower part with cellophane paper that was attached on three sides.

A bulletin-board pond can be used in a variety of ways. For example, as the teacher catches fish, the children name them. All such fish can be attached to the side of the board, eventually allowing for a review of all the fish caught. At other times, two children might play with the display by taking turns fishing for and naming words. With this procedure, one child should be an able reader in order to make certain that words are correctly identified.

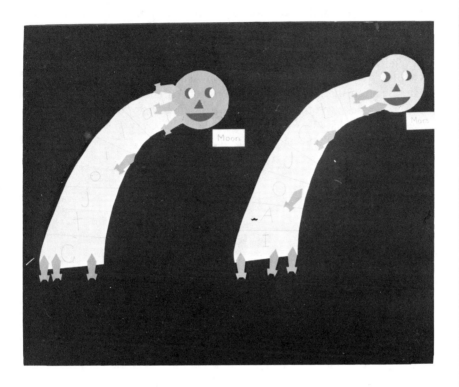

Figure 7–8. Practice in Associating Letters and Sounds

This bulletin-board display took advantage of children's interest in space and exploration. Letters whose sounds had been taught earlier were printed on paths leading to the moon and Mars. (Prior to this, moon, Mars, *and* Mercury *had helped to specify the sound that* m *records.) Children took turns traveling the paths by pointing to each successive letter with a small rocket and by naming a word that began (or ended) with its sound. Correct examples allowed a child to reach the moon or Mars. An incorrect response meant a rocket had lost its way and fallen off into space.*

(Earlier in the year, the same display was used for practice in naming letters. At another time, words were printed on the paths, allowing for reading vocabulary practice.)

While Teacher B's are not as common at the pre-first-grade levels as at the later ones, the likelihood of increased amounts of commercially prepared material for young children could change that. This is why Chapter 7 (and all the previous chapters) highlighted homemade materials that are prepared for particular children. Chapter 7 featured language experience materials, other materials constructed for practice, and bulletin board displays. Although the chapter did not take the position that teachers of young children should bypass all commercial materials, the message of the whole of *Getting Reading Started* is that they should be used only if what they offer (a) will be of interest to young children, and (b) deals with what they need and are ready to learn.

REVIEW

1. Explain the following statement: Covering material and teaching children are not necessarily the same.

2. Let's say that you are a kindergarten teacher who has just been told by your principal that you must use a commercially prepared phonics workbook. Each child will have one. With specific examples, explain why this directive does not make it impossible to have a program in reading that is marked by individualized instruction that has appeal for young children.

3. To show children how useful it is to be able to read, one teacher encouraged them to bring in reading matter of all kinds. Their contributions were displayed on a bulletin board: recipes, candy and gum wrappers, postage stamps, an addressed envelope, menus, labels from canned goods, television schedules, a labeled T-shirt, and a motel brochure. What are some other ways for reminding children of the usefulness of reading ability?

REFERENCES

1. Durkin, Dolores. "What Classroom Observations Reveal about Comprehension Instruction." *Reading Research Quarterly* XIV (1978–79, No. 4), 481–533.
2. EPIE Institute. Report on a National Study of the Nature and Quality of Instructional Materials Most Used by Teachers and Learners. No. 76. New York: EPIE Institute, 1977.

3. Goodlad, John I., and Klein, M. Frances. *Behind the Classroom Door*. Worthington, Ohio: Charles A. Jones Publishing Co., 1970.

4. Smith, Nila B. *Reading Instruction for Today's Children*. Englewood Cliffs, N.J.: Prentice-Hall, 1963.

Index